SURVIVAL SKILLS FOR
freelancers

Tried and tested tips to help you ace
self-employment without burnout

Sarah Townsend

ISBN 978-1-9163715-6-9

sarahtownsendeditorial.co.uk

Cover design: Maple Rock Design, Cheltenham, UK
Page layout: Chapter One Book Production, Knebworth, UK

Praise for Survival Skills for Freelancers

"This book is like having your own personal business mentor. Yes, Sarah gives valuable advice for anyone starting their own business. But, more importantly, she gives an honest and human perspective of her 20 years' experience."

Anna Gunning, copywriter and speaker

"I've been freelancing for over 15 years and I wish I'd read this book on day one. Every page is packed with practical advice and hard-won wisdom. Get it!"

Tom Albrighton, author, Copywriting Made Simple

"A brilliantly relatable, reassuring and comprehensive guide to the world of going freelance. Full of practical tips and real-life examples, it's a guide that holds your hand with compassion and humour through the rocky yet undeniably exciting world of freelancing."

Louise Goss, founder, The Homeworker

"*Survival Skills for Freelancers* beautifully balances the pros, cons and realities of running your own business, and helps you prepare for freelance life. Before you take the leap into self-employment, spend your first few pounds on this book. It'll make every subsequent pound and hour better spent."

Matthew Knight, founder, Leapers

"I wish this book had existed when I set up my business as a freelance creative 14 years ago! Reassuring and honest advice on knowing your value, asking for help and the importance of connection make it a must-read for both new and established freelancers."

Natasha Willmore, creative director, Culpepper & Co

"Genuinely useful advice – delivered in an honest, charming and witty style – with a focus on wellbeing and mental health. An essential read whether you're a new or established freelancer."

Steve Morgan, author, Anti-Sell

"This book could save you hours by providing a path for you to follow on your freelance journey, and helping you to avoid the pitfalls along the way. As you'd expect from a top-class copywriter, it's an easy and enjoyable read, too."

Jonathan Pollinger, social media expert and trainer

"Sarah's book condenses her immense experience into a portable package. With her support you can glide into freelancing and forge a successful new career – or find fresh new ideas to bring into your existing business life."

Leif Kendall, director, ProCopywriters

Contents

Foreword
by Simon Blake OBE

This is a book that every freelancer should know about and read.

Sarah was first recommended to me when I was a new Chief Executive about 15 years ago. We needed someone talented and reliable to help us with our publications. I quickly learned to trust Sarah's approach and her way with words.

She is clear, straightforward, diligent and a joy to work with because she says what she thinks and delivers what she commits to. I was so pleased when Sarah invited me to write this foreword because I know you can trust her advice.

In *Survival Skills for Freelancers*, Sarah has generously shared her 20 years of experience as a freelancer in an easy-to-read, digestible format to help others avoid the pitfalls and mistakes that she and many others have made.

A true myth buster, the book provides practical advice about the nuts and bolts of freelance work, peppered with personal anecdotes, along with wisdom from other freelancers.

Crucially, Sarah provides advice and guidance on managing your own wellbeing and mental health, and avoiding burnout – topics that are all too often overlooked in business books.

This isn't going to be one of those books you read and put on the shelf. Instead, it will be a desk companion you keep popping back to for advice and inspiration.

Props to Sarah for taking the time to share her experience, and to everyone reading it – well done! You found the right book to help you on your way, and I wish you the very best of luck in your freelance endeavours.

Simon Blake OBE
CEO, Mental Health First Aid England
May 2020

Introduction
by Sarah Townsend

My business, Sarah Townsend Editorial Limited, turned 18 in 2017. "You should do something to celebrate!" everyone said. "Great," I thought. "I'll write a blog, sharing all the things that have worked for me in my career, so other people can make **their** freelance businesses more successful!"

By the time I'd finished, my business had been going 20 years.

Being a words person, maths has never been my strong suit – but even I can work out that it took me **two years** to write that post.

Why?

Good question; simple answer.

How in the heck do you cram 20 years of advice into one moderately sized blog post? It simply isn't possible.

Except, as it turned out, it is possible.

Survival Skills for Freelancers: the blog generated an overwhelmingly positive response – and the experience opened my eyes.

People were ready for the truth about self-employment: and they loved the honest, no-frills advice, combined with the heart-on-your-sleeve confessions.

I'd worked damn hard to get to a place where I felt like my success was sustainable. I'd tried things that worked and things that didn't, and learnt a hell of a lot along the way.

I realised I could use my experience to create an indispensable guide to the highs and lows of freelance life. A book containing the sort of advice 29-year-old me would have loved at the start of my own freelance journey.

And here it is.

I hope it helps you to rock the socks off freelance life.

Sarah Townsend
Author

PART ONE

GETTING STARTED

Who should read this book?

While the anecdotes and stories in *Survival Skills for Freelancers* relate to my experiences as a freelance copywriter, the advice is relevant to anyone who's taken – or is thinking of taking – the leap into self-employment.

If you are:

- dreaming of working for yourself but need encouragement to take the first step

- wondering if you've got what it takes to make a success of self-employment

- new to freelance life and want to give your business the best chance of success

- struggling with the isolation and uncertainty of being freelance

- making a good living from your talents, but you need help with the 'running a business' bit

And you want to:

- reduce stress

- earn a good income

- improve your work–life balance

- feel more connected

- avoid overwhelm and burnout

- manage the ups and downs of freelance life

- work how you want, when you want, with clients who appreciate you

… this book is for you.

A note about terminology

Some sectors use the term 'freelancer' more than others – and whether you identify with the term can depend on the job you do and the industry you work in.

You might prefer 'sole-trader', 'consultant', 'entrepreneur', 'solopreneur' or just plain old 'self-employed'.

How does this book work?

Survival Skills for Freelancers contains 20 years' worth of in-depth, super-charged life hacks to help you up your freelance game and get more enjoyment from self-employment.

- It's an honest account of freelance life and the secrets and surprises I've discovered along the way: both the things that worked **and** the things that didn't.

- It busts the myths about the joy and pain of working for yourself – and tells it as it **really** is.

- It's crammed full of personal stories from my own experience, research and resources to help and support you, and tips from the freelance community.

There's no quick-fix cheat sheet, no get-rich-quick scheme and no silver bullet. Instead, I'll help you adopt the mindset you need to achieve your definition of success without neglecting your own wellbeing and mental health.

The structure

As no two journeys to self-employment are the same, I start with the story of how I became a freelancer. I then cover some freelance fundamentals to get you started, before moving on to dispel the eight myths of freelance life.

Each myth section starts with my own brand of heart-on-your-sleeve reality, combined with practical strategies and advice. This is followed by an exercise to help you reflect on – and implement – what you've learned.

Sections entitled **How is it for you?** share experience from other freelancers in the form of mini case studies, and all myth sections end with quotes from the freelance community. Some of the professionals I've quoted are new to the freelance world; others have a ton of solo working experience. But whatever job they do and however long they've worked for themselves, they **all** have valuable advice to share.

The road to self-employment

The freelance dream is often portrayed as:

earning good money doing the thing you love

+

working where you like

+

working how you like

+

working when you like

But the dream of complete control over your workload, salary and schedule is, more often than not, unrealistic.

It's a rare and fortunate freelancer who gets to pick and choose their clients and work from day one. Many of the benefits of working for yourself can only be unlocked by years of hard graft, reputation building and solid experience.

A 2019 survey[1] found that 61% of freelancers work five days a week or more. Many said they work longer hours than they did when they were employed. What's more, 68% are stressed by long working hours and tight deadlines.

You're more likely to be up at the crack of dawn after pulling an all-nighter to cope with a shedload of work – then crying into your soup because you missed out on yet another pitch and don't know where your next paycheque is coming from.

While the reality may not be quite that dramatic, it's important to know the whole truth and nothing but the truth before you take the leap into self-employment.

In 2020, the number of self-employed people in the UK passed 5 million for the first time – and over 2 million of those are freelancers[2].

Despite the growing popularity of freelance life, the harsh truth is that 20% of self-employed businesses don't make it through the first year, while 60% don't survive beyond five years[3].

Yes, working alone can be damn hard. Yet going into self-employment with your eyes wide open gives you a better chance of not becoming one of those statistics.

I'm here to tell you about the reality.

The freelance journey

The path to freelance life is rarely straight.

We don't go through childhood telling our parents and teachers that we want to be a freelancer when we grow up. Few of us leave university and step straight into self-employment. (Though, interestingly, the number of self-employed 16 to 24 year olds has increased a massive 74% since 2014[4].)

It's normal to experiment and stumble around for a bit, trying new things and dipping into different jobs before finding the one thing you want to do – and sticking to it.

Today's focus on following your dreams and pursuing your passions can feel like a lot of pressure – particularly on young people. What if you don't know what your passion is? What if you have lots of passions and don't know which one to choose?

Many people do a job that doesn't suit them for years before realising it's possible to make a living from the thing you love.

Some people don't discover their niche until much later in life, while others never settle on one career.

Some spend years building up a freelance business in their spare time. By the time they're ready to turn their side hustle into a full-time career they have a safety net of clients, contacts and regular work lined up.

For me, being a freelancer was never part of the plan – and so sharing how I got started on my journey to self-employment seems like a good place to start.

The good life

It's human nature that when we see someone with something we want, we're curious as to how they got it. "She's doing all right – what's her secret?"

I'm not the highest earning freelancer. I don't have the most awards. I don't work for Apple, or Innocent, or Nike.

But I make a good living from work I love. I earn enough to invest in my business **and** take holidays, and I (now) make time for life outside the office.

I'm consistently busy. I have a waiting list (usually a pretty healthy one). I delegate and subcontract the tasks I don't enjoy.

I don't advertise. My clients find me, rather than the other way around. What's more, I get to choose projects that excite and inspire me and say no to work that doesn't.

So, how did I get where I am today? And, more importantly, how can **you** get to where I am a whole lot quicker – while avoiding the mistakes I made along the way?

What follows is the story of how I found my way into marketing, and became a freelancer many years later.

Let's start at the beginning...

I never wanted to go to university.

I recall being summoned to see the head of sixth form at Cirencester Deer Park School and being given a lecture on why going straight into employment was a big mistake.

"With your grades, you should be going to university, not going out to work! It's a waste of your education. Study hard, get a degree, and **then** get a job – you can earn so much more with a real qualification under your belt!"

But I didn't **want** a degree, I wanted independence. For me, that independence would come from earning my own money – and my Saturday job serving behind the record counter in Woolworths wouldn't cut it.

In my classic stubborn fashion, I ignored the well-meaning advice of the careers counsellor and school bigwigs and began applying for jobs.

Local insurance companies, Allied Dunbar and Eagle Star, were recruiting school leavers, so I applied and was offered both jobs. I had a decision to make, and so I did what any self-respecting 18-year-old would do... I picked the company with the swankiest office.

While my college friends were off at university and polytechnic getting knee-deep in debt, I was out in the real world (aka Swindon) earning a half-decent wage and – most importantly – gaining experience that would set me up for freelance life. I just didn't know it.

I spent three years working in policy admin at Allied Dunbar. It wasn't the most glamorous or exciting of roles, yet I learnt to use computers, to multitask, to work as part of a team, and to provide great customer service.

I developed a reputation for being the company's "most enthusiastic school leaver" and was soon invited to attend recruitment events, where I'd chat to students about the joys of working in financial services.

I felt like a real-life grown up.

Then, in 1990, I met my ex-husband at a nightclub in Cheltenham. Our relationship developed quickly, and we decided to buy a flat together. Neither of us wanted to live in Swindon, so it seemed obvious that I should resign from my job at Allied Dunbar and once again apply to work at Eagle Star in his home town.

Finding my niche

It's fair to say I fell into marketing.

Fast forward to 1992 and I was happily processing mortgages at Eagle Star Life when rumour spread that the company's marketing department was relocating from London to Cheltenham and was recruiting.

I didn't know a lot about marketing, other than it sounded cool – and I figured I could do it. I was getting married that year and remember trying out my new name and dream job title in a cheery voice inside my head: "Good morning, Sarah Townsend, marketing!"

It felt right. This would be a new me.

I applied for and secured a job as a marketing assistant. After an initial training week in London where I discovered desktop publishing, fonts and the four Ps (product, price, place, promotion) I started my first ever marketing job.

It turned out not all marketing was glamorous. I spent much of those early days writing sales aids on mortality and morbidity, and the cost of delay on pensions. But, when you threw in the occasional trip to our ad agency, Ogilvy & Mather – based in the unspeakably chic Canary Wharf – and the chance to style up the odd photo shoot for the front cover of a glossy product brochure, I was living the dream. And there was so much I wanted to learn!

Luckily, Eagle Star was hot on training and I was sent to the head office of the Chartered Institute of Marketing (expensed travel – swoon!), where I took courses that included everything from proofreading to the snappily titled *Practical Planning and Writing for Print*.

As time went by, I took over responsibility for the company's in-house newsletter and began working on their customer magazine (complete with 200,000 print run – heady stuff!).

Eventually I was promoted to publications controller with my own team, which earned the nickname, The Coloured Pencils.

I interviewed and recruited my own assistant, Sam. She was 20, and it was her first job. Together, Sam and I fought the good fight in the name of grammar: we began using the more modern-looking sentence case for headlines in our staff newsletter, and I convinced my manager that there really was no need for the word doctor to have a capital D on our application forms.

They felt like important battles and, what's more, we were winning.

Where corporate meets agency

These were good times. I worked with some fun people, enjoyed the office banter and seemed to fit in (no small achievement in my life, believe me).

But when you're on the inside of corporate marketing, your out-of-town suppliers seem like the coolest, edgiest people you could ever meet.

For me, no one was cooler than the guys who worked at Specialist – the company that handled the design and publishing of *Eagle Star Magazine*. These were 'the creatives' of legend, and 25-year-old me was in awe.

Each time I met with someone from Specialist, I felt somehow taller, more confident, and more glamorous – as if a little of their creative magic dust had rubbed off on me.

I wanted **in**. I didn't just want to work with them – hell, I wanted to **be** one of them.

Back then, Specialist was populated with designers, editors, and account managers who worked together to create slick-looking magazines that were mailed to their clients' customers.

The company was based in a penthouse office in Clifton, Bristol with these things called 'Apple Macs', and they used acronyms like CMYK and DPS (double-page spread). They had editorial meetings, brainstormed feature ideas, and commissioned real-life journalists, some of whom worked for themselves (an idea that seemed both risky and appealing, even back then).

I loved my job at Eagle Star, but I craved the buzz and magic of agency life. Working for Specialist became my focus. When management decided to cut a third of the marketing department – and offered generous packages for anyone applying for redundancy – I jumped at the chance.

From client side to agency side

I left Eagle Star one Friday in September and started my dream job as an editor and account manager for Specialist the following Monday. (With hindsight, I might have taken at least a long weekend, but hey – live and learn!)

I was given responsibility for four titles: *Eagle Star Magazine*, *Talking Finance* for Allied Dunbar, *Performance* for the GM Card (a collaboration between Vauxhall Motors and HFC Bank), and *Chinthe* for the international oil company, Burmah Castrol.

Despite the comfort-zone factor of continuing to work with Eagle Star, I soon realised there were only so many fresh ways to talk about pensions and life assurance. My true love was *Performance* – a mini mag that quickly became my pride and joy.

The idea of the GM Card was simple: by using the card to pay for purchases, customers earned points they could put towards the cost of a new car. To get people to buy into the dream of owning a Vauxhall, *Performance* was a 'lifestyle' magazine.

This was a whole new concept to me.

We didn't just write about cars or, err, credit cards. Oh no. We wrote about **aspirational stuff** – and I loved it.

Every two months I was responsible for pitching feature ideas to the client in our glass-walled penthouse-office boardroom. Together we'd agree the content of the next issue then head out for a fancy lunch and a large glass of vino.

Each issue of *Performance* contained a celebrity interview, a giveaway (usually a luxury minibreak), a shopping spread, and a feature on the latest Vauxhall vehicle.

But, for me, the real highlight was getting my own editor's welcome message and a headshot in each issue. (I still have a copy. I'm not sure how it's possible to look older at 26 than I did at 40 but, believe me, I pulled it off.)

Language lessons, life lessons

I loved every minute of my time at Specialist. My managing editor, Karen Ellison, was a legend. She and our managing director used to chain smoke their way through every client pitch, but she was talented and funny and creative and a whirlwind of energy.

Karen taught me a lot.

I remember writing my first lifestyle feature for Iceland magazine (the frozen food store, not the country). I'd peppered it with 'smiled Phil' and 'laughed Sue'. She taught me to keep it simple, and always use 'said'. I learned the difference between a hyphen and an en dash, and that you never (ever) put a comma before a postcode.

Karen also takes the credit for teaching me that possessive 'its' doesn't have an apostrophe. (I'm not proud to admit that I was 26 before I learned that it was wrong to write 'the dog wagged it's tail', but I was educated in the 70s when grammar was out of style and freeform writing was the order of the day. Course, if I'd gone to university…)

A new life – and a new life

I'd worked at Specialist for three fun-packed years when I became pregnant. I was living in Gloucester and working in Clifton, and while I knew I didn't have it in me to be a full-time, stay-at-home mum, I also knew I had no intention of coming back to work full-time or commuting to Bristol with a baby in nursery back home.

I spoke to my managing director about the idea of returning to work part-time and was politely shut down: "You're an account manager – you can't expect your clients to understand that you only work three days a week!"

While I was disappointed, I wasn't surprised. This was the 90s, and flexible hours and remote working had yet to gain popularity. (Hell, we'd only just got the internet! We had one computer in the whole agency that contained this dark magic known as the World Wide Web, which we could access using something called Netscape Navigator. It was scary and exhilarating in equal measure.)

Karen suggested the idea of working freelance, and said they would help me out by sending me magazines to proofread. This seemed like a fair compromise, so after a lot of careful thought, I decided to go for it.

In early 1999, I left Specialist on maternity leave. I spent most of my leave designing my own letterhead, comp slips, and business cards, and drafting and posting letters to local companies I knew I could help.

My daughter was born in May and started part-time at a nursery just down the road a few months later.

And the rest, as they say, is history.

Because everything that happened in the 20 years that followed has shaped the advice in this book.

I created my freelance career with very little guidance, **but you don't have to.**

So, dig in and let's start with the basics.

1   How are we doing? Leapers research into freelancing and mental health: leapers.co/huru/report/

2   Office for National Statistics, Labour Market Overview, March 2020: ons.gov.uk/employmentandlabourmarket/peopleinwork/employmentandemployeetypes/bulletins/employmentintheuk/march2020

3   One-fifth of self-employed sole traders don't survive one year, and the majority don't survive five: Institute for Fiscal Studies: ifs.org.uk/publications/14243

4   Going solo: The rise of self-employment: bbc.co.uk/news/business-44887623

PART TWO

THE BASICS

The fundamentals
of freelancing

Ask 100 freelancers how they'd define success, and you'll get 100 different answers.

If you're a parent, success may involve creating a flexible, fulfilling career that fits around school hours and term time, so you can enjoy your children growing up.

Perhaps to you, success means swapping corporate life for a higher purpose, and using your talents and skills to help an ethical or charitable cause that complements your values.

Or perhaps you're driven by a desire to be debt-free and to own your own home.

Success to me means I'm financially secure. Being a single parent for more than 12 years has made financial independence and the ability to provide stability for my children even more important to me.

But it's not just about the money.

I get to pick and choose who I work with. I have the time and resources to do the things I want to do. Most of all, success to me means I get to do a job I love – day in, day out.

It took me the best part of 15 years to get good at the things in this book. My aim is to help you achieve your own definition of success in a **lot** less time.

The qualities for solo success

If you're thinking of making the leap from a regular monthly income to the uncertainty of going solo, there are some important things to consider.

Not just the obvious, like "what do I charge?", "how do I attract the right clients?" or "how do I market my business?". While these are all vital questions, I'm talking about the dirty, gritty, soul-searching stuff. The "am I really cut out for self-employment?" delving you need to do before you start.

I only have experience of life as a freelance copywriter, but the same issues apply to any self-employed role – creative or coach, designer or developer, personal trainer or photographer.

Have you got what it takes?

There are numerous qualities that will help you succeed as a freelancer. It goes without saying that you need to be great at what you do – but skills and talent alone are no guarantee of success.

If you're currently employed and considering self-employment, it pays to do your homework.

Before you get carried away in the dream of working for yourself, start by making a list of all the things you like about being employed. While the desire to go it alone can be strong and the benefits clear, it's easy to overlook the advantages of having a steady job – and you need to be prepared to let these things go.

First, there are the financial rewards, such as a pension, sick pay, holiday pay, parental leave, bonuses, life assurance, paid overtime, and, above all, a regular income.

Then you have the benefits of being part of a team: the office banter, the coffee-point catch ups with colleagues, sharing accountability, and a sense of contributing to something bigger.

Some people need to be managed. They need tasks to be allocated with a clear list of priorities, and both encouragement and incentive to achieve those tasks on time. Solo workers need to be self-starters with the motivation and drive to do these things themselves.

Finding your strengths

When I started the process of writing this book, I asked the freelance community on Twitter a question: "To succeed as a freelancer, you need to be…". What follows are some of the most common answers:

tenacious	outgoing	enthusiastic
driven	ambitious	sociable
determined	patient	extrovert
motivated	organised	curious
flexible	courageous	persistent
reliable	optimistic	disciplined
authentic	confident	thick-skinned
creative	resilient	responsible

If you've done all the thinking and you're convinced you're ready to follow the freelance path, these qualities can help to increase your chances of success.

Don't be disheartened if you don't tick every box. It's entirely possible to succeed in the freelance world with just a handful of these traits.

However, the more qualities you have, the better your chances of surviving and thriving as a solo worker. If you don't identify with **any** of them, it may be worth thinking again about whether going it alone is the right decision for you.

Just as certain characteristics can help smooth your path to freelance success, others can be a real obstacle. For example, being terrible at time management, dreadfully disorganised, or a procrastinator at heart can make life difficult if you're not prepared to work at them.

On a brighter note, you may find some traits that hold you back when you're working as part of a team are a distinct advantage when you're going it alone.

For example, having a high need for control can be a useful asset for a freelancer, when you're responsible for making your own decisions, day in, day out – but may cause friction in the world of employment where it's important to take other people's opinions and needs into account.

Knowing your weaknesses

Two of the traits that cropped up again and again in my research were **patience** and **thick skin**.

While I agree that both qualities are beneficial in many ways, I have neither. If I decide to do something, nothing gets in my way. I want results, and I want them now. (I've been described as a force of nature on more than one occasion. I'm not sure it was meant as a compliment.)

As for being thick-skinned... I couldn't be less so. When I started my freelance journey, people told me I'd develop a thick skin over time. They were wrong.

I recently read a book called *The Highly Sensitive Person*, by Elaine N Aron. The book starts with a quiz to help you identify how sensitive you are. I scored 19 out of 23.

It's safe to say that I identify as being both highly sensitive **and** highly impatient – but I'm okay with that. Most weaknesses can be reframed as strengths. Impatient people make things happen, and they can be great at encouraging other people to get things done. Sensitive people can be great listeners – a crucial skill for freelancers – and are often highly attuned to important signals from the world around them.

Would life be easier without weaknesses? Sure. But they haven't held me back or prevented me from becoming a successful freelancer – and they won't hold you back, either.

Dealing with rejection

Whether you'd consider yourself to be thick-skinned or otherwise, criticism and rejection can be a cold, hard fact of freelance life.

Back in the 1990s, my brother-in-law was involved in a pyramid selling scheme. The walls of the house he shared with his wife at the time were plastered with motivational posters saying things like "Big money moves slow," "ABC: Always Be Closing" and "The NOs don't count!".

But when you're responsible for paying the mortgage or the rent each month, the NOs do count! Every client that doesn't convert, every email that goes unanswered, and every proposal that's rejected can increase stress and knock your confidence.

Having the ability to take criticism professionally, not personally, is a useful skill for anyone to cultivate – regardless of whether or not they're self-employed.

Of course, there are many ways in which rejection really **isn't** personal. Perhaps your timing is wrong, your prices are too high (or too low), your approach isn't compatible, or you're simply the wrong fit for either the job or the client (more on that in **myth five**).

You can't go solo without putting yourself out there in the metaphorical firing line and being vulnerable – and if you're not emotionally resilient, your mental health can suffer as a result.

Boosting emotional resilience

The good news is that emotional resilience isn't something you are or aren't born with: it's something you can learn. According to UK mental health charity, Mind, developing emotional resilience can help you deal with pressure, and reduce the impact of stress.

Your resilience is your ability to bounce back from difficulty – and it determines how well you adapt to challenging circumstances, while maintaining a stable mental wellbeing. The more resilient you are, the better equipped you'll be to deal with the relentless ups and downs of freelance life.

Mind's tips for boosting your emotional resilience fall into four categories:

- Make some lifestyle changes.

- Look after your physical health.

- Give yourself a break.

- Build your support network.

Each of these strategies is covered in this book – and you can read more of Mind's suggestions on their website[1].

While I don't like waiting for things to happen in their own time, I'm well aware of my impatience. Being aware of your weaknesses makes you better equipped to work on them. And while you may be completely comfortable with the qualities you lack, it's often in your power to develop these areas if you know there's room for improvement.

Self-help books, training courses, coaching, and counselling such as cognitive behavioural therapy (CBT) can provide help if you need it.

Freelance life is not for the faint-hearted. But if you're organised, tenacious, disciplined and driven, it can be downright brilliant.

Success vs struggle

In an article for writingonglass.com[2], Tia Meyers, founder of 42,000-strong Facebook community, Freelancing Females lists self-esteem and a willingness to network as two important differences between the freelancers who thrive and those who struggle to find clients – particularly for women.

"There are a lot of different factors, but one is self-esteem. A lot of women in the beginning are very nervous about calling themselves a freelancer on LinkedIn or telling people that they're freelancing now from their previous job.

"That's one of the biggest things in being successful. Getting yourself out there is one of the most important things you can do as a freelancer, because once you get the word out there, people are going to recommend you."

Finding your personality profile

If, like me, you're fascinated by what makes people tick – or simply interested in gaining a better understanding of your own strengths and weaknesses – you might want to learn more about personality profiling.

Two of the most well-known profiling tools are the Myers-Briggs Type Indicator® (MBTI)[3] and DiSC®[4]. Both ask questions to establish your personal preferences.

MBTI testing is based on the psychological types identified by Carl Jung. The analysis covers four categories:

- extroversion (E) vs introversion (I)

- sensing (S) vs intuition (N)

- thinking (T) vs feeling (F)

- judging (J) vs perceiving (P)

By expressing a preference in each category, you end up with one of 16 MBTI personality types, which is expressed as a code with four letters.

When I took an MBTI assessment many years ago, I scored highly in extroversion. But it's worth mentioning that if you identify as being introverted – as many freelancers do – you may find days filled with meetings, networking, conferences and phone calls draining. If this sounds like you, acknowledge that you need quiet and alone time to recharge and perform at your best, and build this into your day.

DiSC profiling was created by William Moulton Marston – a lawyer and psychologist, who not only invented the lie detector but also created Wonder Woman.

Marston's DiSC model measures your tendencies and preferences and provides an outline of your expected behaviour in various situations, such as how you respond to challenges and how you influence others.

The four categories – D, I, S, and C – are based on a four-square grid. Those who fall into the left-hand categories (D and C) tend to be task-focused, and those in the right-hand categories (I and S) tend to be people-focused.

The categories are broken down further, with D and I people being fast-paced and outgoing, and S and C people being slower and more introverted.

- D: results-driven, strong-willed, independent, assertive, decisive and forceful

- I: energetic, outgoing, enthusiastic, persuasive, optimistic and creative

- S: dependable, caring, agreeable, supportive, calm and patient

- C: cautious, persistent, perfectionist, data-oriented, analytical and diplomatic

When I took a DiSC assessment back in 2018, I scored exceptionally highly in the D category and moderately highly in the I category. I found the results uncannily accurate. Colleagues and friends who've taken a DiSC assessment agree that it's given them some useful insights into their strengths and weaknesses.

Finally, Gretchen Rubin – author of *The Happiness Project* – developed the concept of **The Four Tendencies** to provide insight into how you respond to expectations.

Rubin claims that knowing your tendency can help you make better decisions, meet both deadlines and promises to yourself, suffer less stress, and engage more deeply with others. Her quick and simple quiz[5] will tell you whether you're an upholder, questioner, obliger, or rebel. (Much as I long to be a rebel, I'm an upholder – again, eerily accurate.)

These tests aren't designed to measure or summarise every element of your personality, but they may be useful if you're interested in learning more about the ways in which you're likely to react to the challenges of freelance life.

After all, you're going to be spending a lot of time in your own company, so you'll be getting to know yourself pretty well one way or another!

---

1   Mind: how to manage stress: mind.org.uk/information-support/types-of-mental-health-problems/stress/developing-resilience/

2   Writing on Glass interview with Tia Meyers, founder of Freelancing Females: writingonglass.com/content/freelancing-females

3   Myers-Briggs Type Indicator (MBTI): myersbriggs.org

4   DiSC personality profiling: discprofile.com

5   Gretchen Rubin's Four Tendencies quiz: quiz.gretchenrubin.com/

Time out...

Spend some time thinking about your strengths and weaknesses. List the qualities you believe will help you become a successful freelancer, and those that might hold you back.

Are there areas you'd like to work on? How could you do this?

It's just as important to recognise, reflect on and celebrate your strengths (more on this in **myth eight**). Take time to do this, and don't just focus on the areas in which you're lacking.

The practicalities of self-employment

Having looked at the personal qualities needed to make a success of solo working, it's time to think about the practical stuff.

To survive and thrive in the freelance world, you'll need:

- A business name.

- A dedicated space to work in.

- Savings to get you through the inevitable dry spells.

- The tools, technology and equipment you need to do your job.

- A brand, to help your business stand out from the competition.

- A website, to represent your business online.

- A business bank account.

Depending on what sector you work in and what job you do, you may also need:

- A business plan[1].

- Business insurance.

- A pension.

- A contract to cover you should things go wrong (see **references**).

- Transport, such as a works van.

Many of these are covered in more detail in the pages and chapters that follow.

The secret to working from home

Working freelance doesn't necessarily mean being home-based, and I cover some alternatives to working from home in **myth one**. If you **are** planning on working from home, there are some important steps you can take to make it work for you:

1. *Introduce routine*

2. *Keep moving*

3. *Claim your space*

4. *Avoid distractions*

5. *Stay focused*

6. *Manage your time*

1. *Introduce routine*

It's easy for work and home life to blur if you don't have clear boundaries around when work stops, and home life begins.

Both boundaries and routine are key to achieving a healthy work–life balance and making a success of working from home.

Aim to start and end your day at a set time and schedule regular breaks. If you've come to self-employment from corporate life, consider dedicating the equivalent of your commuting time to reading, catching up on inspiring podcasts or audio books, or listening to music that lifts your mood.

Build in time to take lunch away from your desk, and eat a healthy and nutritious meal to set you up for the afternoon. Aim to take an outdoor break for fresh air and exercise, whatever the weather.

Over time you'll learn when and how you're at your most productive, and you can use this knowledge to structure your day. (More on this in **myth seven.**)

2. *Keep moving*

Most of us spend way too much time being inactive. We switch between time spent sleeping to eating breakfast in front of the TV, sitting in front of a computer, sitting down for dinner, then relaxing in front of the TV to unwind at the end of the day.

With health experts describing sitting as the new smoking[2], and advice to strive for 10,000 steps each day, there's no shortage of reasons why inactivity is the enemy. But it's all too easy to find yourself stuck in a sedentary lifestyle if you don't make a determined effort to move – and regularly!

Instead of spending your day hunched over your laptop, take regular breaks away from your desk and stretch out those muscles. Take your phone calls standing up. Pace circuits of your home while you chat to clients and colleagues.

Set an hourly alarm on your phone or wear a fitness tracker or smart watch that'll give you a nudge to get moving. (My Apple Watch is great for this. It even gives me regular reminders to breathe deeply. It may sound obvious, but it helps me calm down when I'm stressed out.)

If you're using the Pomodoro time management technique described later in this chapter, use your five-minute breaks to get up and shake off any tension in your muscles.

There's no shortage of websites sharing simple and effective stretches you can do at your desk. Alternatively, take a brisk walk around the block, go for a swim in your lunch break, or put on some loud music and dance around your office. It all helps to keep the joints moving and the creative juices flowing.

Freelance Pilates instructor, Russ Jones-Walker, recommends drinking plenty of water – but not just because of the obvious hydration benefits. "Keeping a pint of fresh water on your desk at all times is a great way of making sure you keep moving. You'll be up and down for regular loo breaks, and to refill your glass."

3. *Claim your space*

Journalist and presenter, Louise Goss, agrees that loneliness is one of the biggest challenges for work-from-home freelancers: "Isolation and the lack of social interaction are two of the hardest things about working from home, especially if you're more familiar with an office environment.

"As soon as I tell anyone I run my business from home, I get to hear about how lucky I have it: a lie-in, the lack of commute, wearing PJs all day, no office politics. They don't always understand the reality. No commute means no boundary between life at work and life at home. Wearing PJs doesn't get me into working mode, and lack of office politics means there's no one else around. And that can be tough."

Louise set up the popular blog and magazine, *The Homeworker*[3], to address the issues facing people who work from home and to provide support and advice. It deals with many of the subjects covered in this book, such as coping with isolation and self-doubt, and provides tips on issues such as mindset, your home workspace and productivity.

Not everyone is lucky enough to have a spare room they can use as a home office, but even if space is tight, there's plenty you can do to create a dedicated workspace in your home. A supportive, adjustable chair, good natural light, and a clutter-free table or desk should be top of your list.

Whether you choose to work from your dining room table, a quiet corner of your living room, or get creative with cupboard space, set some rules around the places in your home that are work-free zones for the sake of your family and relationships.

4. *Avoid distractions*

Sometimes it's easier to put things off than bite the bullet and get started. It's a fact of freelance life. But, if we're not careful, we can find our attention scattered by a dozen distractions.

We're all different. I know freelancers who can't work without the buzz of daytime television in the background, whereas I can't even listen to a song with lyrics without losing focus! Whichever camp you fall into, schedule time where distractions and interruptions are minimised, and you can focus on the task at hand.

Step away from the TV remote, stay off social media, disable pop-up notifications, and develop the discipline to stop checking your email every few minutes.

Instead of feeling you need to answer every message immediately, take back control by crafting a carefully worded out-of-office response, and check your messages just a couple of times a day.

As well as giving you valuable time and headspace to focus on your most important tasks, this lets your clients know that you take your work seriously.

While autoresponders are effective for both email and Facebook Messenger, they don't cover the clients and colleagues who text, WhatsApp or DM on LinkedIn, Twitter, and Instagram. Allocate certain times of day that you'll check for messages, and avoid answering enquiries out of hours. It sets a precedent you may not want – or be able – to stick to.

With working from home comes another kind of distraction: household chores. You can choose to look at these in one of two ways:

- As distracting jobs that you don't touch until you've clocked off for the day.

- As valuable thinking/stretching/stepping-away-from-the-laptop time.

I fall into the latter category. Below, I recommend the Pomodoro Technique. I use my Pomodoro breaks to load and unload my dishwasher, feed my cats, or put on a wash. Not only is this a good way of getting up and moving, but it also means you don't finish your working day only to find a pile of outstanding chores waiting for you!

5. *Stay focused*

If you lack the iron will needed to stop yourself checking social media repeatedly, and you can't simply switch off your wifi, there are plenty of internet blocking apps out there that are designed to prevent you from scratching that itch.

There's no doubt that technology and the internet are a godsend when we're in control of them. But we're all guilty of multi-screening – and it's far too easy to fall down rabbit holes and lose concentration.

Today's culture implies that we should all be experts at juggling and plate spinning – and I'm not talking about circus skills. Yet far from being a sign of efficiency, multitasking makes busy fools of us all.

Studies conducted by Stanford University[4] claim we are suffering from an epidemic of multitasking, and research has found that constant task switching can significantly reduce productivity.

What we describe as multitasking is simply jumping back and forth between tasks, and it could be said to be the opposite of the flow state that's covered in **myth seven**.

Rather than focusing attention on doing one job well, hopping from one thing to another means we make more mistakes, waste time, and lose track of where we started.

6. *Manage your time*

It's a lot easier to focus when you feel more in control of your time.

When I need to stay focused on a task, I use the Pomodoro Technique[5].

If you're not familiar with it, the Pomodoro Technique is a simple and effective way to boost your productivity and improve focus. It uses a timer – traditionally tomato-shaped, hence the name – to break the day into manageable chunks of time.

The idea is that you set the timer for 25 minutes and focus completely and utterly on the task at hand. When the timer goes off, take a five-minute break. Step away from your laptop, make yourself a drink, do some stretches… or all three. The idea is to take a longer break after four timed stints.

You might find you prefer to set the timer for a longer period – 40-minute stints work best for me when I'm focused on writing, for example. Experiment until you find a routine that works for you.

What's next?

We've looked at the route to freelance life. We've covered some of the characteristics and skills that can help you succeed at self-employment. And we've touched on the practicalities of working from home.

Next, it's time to bust the myths.

---

1   The fact that the need for a business plan is on my 'nice to have' list instead of my 'must have' list may be controversial. But, as I've never had one it would be hypocritical of me to tell you it's essential.

2   Why too much sitting is bad for your health: nhs.uk/live-well/exercise/why-sitting-too-much-is-bad-for-us/

3   *The Homeworker*: thehomeworker.com/

4   Multitasking and productivity: Eyal Ophir, Clifford Nass and Anthony D Wagner, *Cognitive control in media multitaskers*, via PNAS.org/content/106/37/15583.full

5   The Pomodoro Technique: https://francescocirillo.com/pages/pomodoro-technique

FREELANCER FEEDBACK…

One of the most important lessons in *Survival Skills for Freelancers* is the need to find your people. To demonstrate the power of the freelance community, I've included quotes and feedback from other freelance professionals throughout the book.

Some of these opinions are direct responses to questions I've asked on Twitter; others came about through face-to-face conversations, or the many video calls I had during the process of writing the book.

Some of the people I've quoted are brand new to the freelance world; others have a ton of experience of solo working. But whatever job they do, whatever industry they work in, and however long they've worked for themselves, they **all** have valuable advice to share.

Below are just a few responses from the Twitter community, to the question: "To make it as a successful freelancer, you need…"

"Motivation. Determination. Thick skin. A desire to keep improving. A mentor. A community. To give more than you take. To work hard and be nice."

@thatcontentshed

"A healthy work–life balance to avoid burnout."

@lostandfoundcc

"Success as a freelancer is not just about being talented. It takes toughness and discipline. You must put in the hard work and seek answers yourself. You have to truly believe in yourself and master the technique of selling yourself to potential clients."

@CatOlsonWriting

"To be clear on what you don't do."

@SuzannaJackson1

"Curiosity:
- About trying new things, experimenting, seeing what works.
- About what your clients (and their customers) think, want, and need."

*@louiseshanahan_*

"Being able to ask what some might consider stupid questions – or knowing where or whom to ask – is vital. In a team, you'd have people to go to. As a freelancer, you often have to find different ways to ask."

@nijomo

"Pals! Lovely lovely freelancey pals. Internet-based or otherwise. Vital."

@re_scrawl

"Remember that you are, above all, there to save people time. Being able to nail a brief is the minimum requirement. What gets you booked is being low maintenance, diplomatic, good with clients, setting high standards for yourself, and having zero ego."

@MattPhilCarver

PART THREE

BUSTING THE MYTHS
OF FREELANCE LIFE

MYTH ONE

"I like my own company.
I don't need anyone else."

The reality

Being a solo worker doesn't mean going it alone

Let's face it – you need plenty of grit, drive, and determination even to make the decision to go it alone.

- Perhaps you were – or are – drawn to the idea of going solo because you're fiercely independent and love your own company.

- Perhaps you've never fitted into a group working environment, and you don't consider yourself to be a team player.

- Perhaps you've experienced bad management that borders on bullying and you've had enough.

But however tired you are of office politics – and however comfortable you are in your own company – there will be times when you'll miss the buzz and the banter of being part of a team.

Nothing prepares you for the loneliness and isolation of going solo, and it's even harder if you've no one who understands the challenges.

If your partner, your family and your close friends are all employed, they may see freelance life as a bit of a soft option. They've no grasp of the fact that freelancing is as real a job as any stable 9 to 5 number – just harder.

- We're responsible for finding our own clients, managing our own workload, earning our own income and paying our own rent.

- We don't get sick pay, parental leave, pensions, holiday pay or any of the many benefits of working for a large company.

- We can't just close the door and walk away at 5pm, even if we want to.

- And it's difficult to prevent the boundary between work and home becoming blurred, however hard you try.

Whatever square of the freelance board game you're currently on, finding your people can make your working life a **lot** more enjoyable.

Eat, sleep, work, repeat

Freelance community, Leapers – who describe themselves as 'the team for those without a team' – carried out a study of the impact of freelance life on mental health.

Of the 500 freelancers they surveyed, 60% said they don't mind working alone, while a significant 40% admitted they struggle with the isolation[1].

We human beings are social creatures with a fundamental need to feel valued and to belong. If you live alone and work from home, it's all too easy for days to pass since you last had contact with another person.

You find yourself initiating conversation with strangers while out walking the dog, or popping into Sainsbury's just to chat with the guy behind the cheese counter.

It's all too easy to feel trapped inside your own head, not to mention stumbling into your office and starting your day without taking care of yourself and your wellbeing.

Left unchecked, the loneliness and unpredictability of freelance life can be a recipe for mental health issues such as anxiety and depression.

Out of office…

When I started my freelance career in 1999, email was new, coworking didn't exist, and today's popular social media platforms were a mere twinkle in the eye of a Harvard dropout – in fact, there was barely an internet!

I spent the first 15 years of freelance life stuck in my office, home alone, with only my cats for company. By the weekend – hell, by the end of each day – cabin fever had set in. I was climbing the walls and chewing the ears off anyone who'd listen.

I may have been late to the party (in my defence, there **was** no party in those early years) but discovering the support that's available through social media, networking, and events – not to mention the joys of working in a decent coffee shop or coworking space – was an eye opener.

The lounge bar at my gym quickly became my second office when I realised I could get good coffee, stable wifi, free heating, and the buzz of being around other people without the constant interruptions of working in an office.

HOW IS IT FOR YOU?

Finding likeminded individuals to cowork, collaborate, and share with can be a game changer – and self-employed magician, Richard Parsons, agrees. In fact, he goes as far as to attribute his success to the connections he's made along the way.

"I can sum up my growth and development as a business in one word – community. It's so easy to create online connections with your industry peers using social media... but it's even more important to take those connections offline and make the effort to meet in person," Richard says.

"I regularly meet other professional magicians, wedding industry freelancers, and event gurus to exchange ideas, resolve problems, and support each other. And I'm proud to say many of these connections have become good friends."

So, choose wisely. Pick the people who inspire and support you, who lift your energy with their positivity and ideas, and who make you laugh – not the energy vampires who flatten you with their gripes about how hard it is to be your own boss. No one needs that.

As John Donne famously said, "No man is an island." However independent, self-contained, and introverted you are, everyone – **even you** – needs to know they're not alone.

And you're not.

Common ground is a great starting point for lasting friendship and support – and it's out there. You just need to know where to look.

---

1   How are we doing? Leapers research into freelancing and mental health: leapers.co/huru/report/

The advice

Everybody needs somebody

Knowing you're not alone – and that others understand, and share, your experience – can help you maintain a positive mindset and enjoy your working life.

According to research[1], 58% of freelancers feel they'd benefit from connecting with others in similar situations. And there are three places to find those connections:

1. *Coworking spaces*

2. *Online communities*

3. *Networking groups*

Let's look at each of these in detail.

1. *Coworking spaces and coffee shop working*

New flexible workspaces are opening in many towns and cities with a regularity that could rival Starbucks or Subway.

According to an article in the *Telegraph*[2], coworking locations in London alone totalled 11.5 million square feet in 2018 – and the number is on the rise, with a new workspace opening in the capital every five days[3].

While you don't need to be a freelancer to use a coworking space – shared work zones attract flexible workers of all kinds – many freelancers find shared working gives them the lifeline they need to overcome the isolation that comes with the job title.

Freelancers who use coworking spaces get a lot more from doing so than desk space. When I asked my freelance community what they enjoy about coworking, responses included the buzz, camaraderie and chat, opportunities for collaboration, improved productivity, mutual support, the chance to network, less loneliness, a vital boundary between work and home, and great coffee!

Claire Storey, founder of Gloucestershire-based coworking space, The Workplace, agrees: "Our members don't just come here to work – they can do that at home. They come here to meet interesting, motivated people. When I set up The Workplace back in 2017, I thought I was in the business of providing desk space for people who had none. I now realise it's not desk space we offer – it's headspace.

"Most people who work here struggle to work from home, and they all think they're alone in this. Everyone loves the idea of having flexible working hours, but the dream and the reality don't match up for most people. Both efficiency and happiness drop dramatically once the loneliness kicks in. Most of our members have a workspace at home but prefer to pay to share an office with others as it makes them happier and more productive."

But it's not essential to join an organised coworking space to get a sense of community. Just as I enjoy the buzz and relative anonymity that comes from working at my gym, you may prefer to mix it up by trying different cafés or coffee shops (which have the added advantage of being free – refreshments aside).

The cost of company

Finding the right working environment can make a big difference to your productivity, motivation, and wellbeing, so check out a few local venues to see what feels right.

Charging structures vary and you'll need to find one that suits your budget, which may be limited when you're starting out.

Some coworking spaces operate on a pay-as-you-go basis (sometimes called hot-desking) where you can drop in and use the facilities when you need to. (An appealing idea for the more commitment-phobic among you!)

Others work on a membership basis and charge a fixed fee, depending on how many days you need a desk each week or month.

Ultimately, it doesn't matter how funky the furnishings or how good the coffee – it's the people who make a coworking space what it is, so it's worth taking the time to find the right one for you.

Like most things in life, coworking isn't for everyone. A small number of people I spoke to said they find shared working noisy and distracting. Others who spend a lot of their working day on the phone needed complete quiet to focus. (If you're someone who needs silence to do your best work, consider investing in some noise-cancelling headphones.)

If you're set on giving up the long commute and parking agony, and you favour the short walk to your upstairs office instead, you may prefer to find your freelance community online.

2. *Online communities*

Technology and the internet have led to a surge in remote working. The digital nomads who work in far-away places have the same need for connection as those who work from home day in, day out – and online communities and podcasts provide that.

The growing popularity of Facebook groups is proving to be a lifeline to solo workers. Groups such as Freelance Heroes, Being Freelance and Freelancing Females exist to provide advice, support, and camaraderie for the freelance community (see **references** for more details).

There are groups for all industries (chefs, PRs, translators, web designers and developers just for starters) geographical groups (from Freelance Jobs Philippines to the Stroud Freelance Sisterhood) and some serious niches (freelance grooms, anyone?!) – and new ones are emerging all the time.

Of course, if there's nothing for your particular field or area, there's nothing to stop you setting up a group yourself.

Group members share their experiences and post questions, challenges and suggestions, and the community responds with help, support and advice. As with most things in life, you get out of online communities what you put in – so dig in, introduce yourself, browse their posts, give generously, and don't self-promote unless you're invited to!

Once you've established yourself as an active member of your online community, and become known as friendly, reliable and someone who knows their stuff, you may even begin to get referrals and business as a result.

But, while these groups exist primarily on Facebook, this isn't the only place to find your online community. Twitter hashtags such as #FreelanceHeroes #FreelanceChat and #ContentClubUK have their own dedicated hours for virtual get-togethers and support (though you can use them at any time to find your people) and you don't have to look far to find likeminded, supportive individuals on Instagram, or even LinkedIn.

HOW IS IT FOR YOU?

Videographer and audio producer, Steve Folland, took the leap into freelance life in 2014. "I made the decision to go freelance so that I could be at home to look after our children. I wasn't used to the isolation, so I went looking for ways to connect with other freelancers and found nothing."

Steve set up popular podcast, **Being Freelance** back in 2015, and the Being Freelance Community Facebook group in 2019. Over 200 podcast episodes later, Being Freelance has a truly global audience, and reaches solo workers as far afield as Haiti, Ghana, Panama and St Lucia.

Meanwhile, in the US, New York-based Tia Meyers set up **Freelancing Females** in 2017, after realising there was no community or safe space dedicated to supporting women in her situation. She established the group to redefine the 9 to 5 and provide a supportive community for women who've taken the leap into freelance life.

Described by *Forbes* magazine as, "A destination for female freelancers to find camaraderie and get paid what they deserve," what began as a Facebook group with a few friends has quickly grown into an active global community, with between 100 and 150 women joining the group each day[4].

It's entirely possible to create great real-life friendships from the people you meet online. #FreelanceHeroesDay and #copywritersunite are just two examples of communities that spill out into socials and conferences where freelancers get to meet in person.

Fellow copywriter, Amy Boylan, summed this up beautifully after a 2019 conference, when she said, "You all take the lonely out of working alone for me, and it's genuine because it works fab in person too."

3. *Networking groups and events*

It takes time to build and nurture connections that can lead to new clients and new business. But, if you're prepared to put the effort in, networking events can be a great place to start. Networking can be a lifeline for the home-based freelancer – as well as a great source of new clients and colleagues – and it's not as scary as you may think.

I confess, the idea of networking used to bring me out in a rash. There was nothing I dreaded more. So much so, that for the first 15 years of my freelance career I did no networking whatsoever.

Having to sell my services to complete strangers? No way, José. Standing in front of a room full of serious, suit-wearing strangers, talking about my business until the timer busted me for rambling? No thanks! Or worse – drying up before the two minutes were up! Imagine the shame.

Then I discovered that not all networking is the same – and that the secret to enjoying it was to find the groups and events that fit my business and personality. Now I network for the connection as much as anything else. For me, it's always been about meeting likeminded people, not indulging in pushy sales pitches.

"I'm a freelancer – get me out of here!"

Even the most introverted of freelancers can benefit from the human connection that comes from putting themselves out there.

If the idea of standing up to deliver a two-minute pitch leaves you cold, check out some of the low-key, informal events out there.

These often include a helpful talk from an expert followed by casual chatting over coffee, and can be a great place to get started.

If you hate small talk, and the thought of chatting about your own business feels salesy and uncomfortable, focus on asking the other person questions instead of talking about yourself.

It can take time to find the right crowd. Try asking the freelance communities online for recommendations in your local area, or check out Facebook Events, Eventbrite or meetup.com for inspiration.

Whether you prefer the commitment of a structured group that meets for breakfast each week and relies on mutual referrals, a casual 'drinks after work' crowd, or a mastermind group of likeminded solo-workers for accountability and encouragement, there really is something out there for everyone. Be prepared to experiment, and don't be put off if the first networking events you try aren't for you.

The value of know, like, and trust

Of course, there's a big side benefit to all this connecting, and it goes far beyond confronting isolation. Each new connection you make has the potential to blossom into a relationship that can support and grow your business.

It's human nature that we're more likely to recommend someone we know, and to buy from someone we like and trust. Your clients don't want to work with you because you're the best in your field. They want to work with you because they like you, you're reliable and easy to get along with, and you show a genuine interest in their business.

So, be prepared to give more than you take, and put time, energy, and effort into creating and nurturing your new community.

Whether you join a networking group or professional body, find a thriving coworking space, mix it up by attending various events or simply go all-out on social media doesn't matter. The support you'll get from finding your people – and the boost to your business as a result – can make an enormous difference to your enjoyment of freelance life.

1   How are we doing? Leapers research into freelancing and mental health: leapers.co/huru/report/

2   Is the coworking trend here to stay? telegraph.co.uk/business/ready-and-enabled/cost-efficiency/coworking/

3   London leads the way in coworking: workplaceinsight.net/london-leads-the-way-in-a-rapid-rise-of-flexible-office-spaces/

4   Forbes interview with founder of Freelancing Females, Tia Meyers: forbes.com/sites/stephanienewman/2018/07/08/how-this-freelancer-built-a-10000-person-facebook-group-in-1-year/#550fa6217b95

Time out...

Think about the kind of support that's missing from your freelance day.

Where could you go to find what you need?

Ask freelance friends and colleagues who they turn to when they need advice, and who supports them when they're struggling.

Can they recommend a real-life networking event, local coworking space, Facebook group, or virtual support through Twitter or Instagram?

Experiment until you find an approach that works for you.

FREELANCER FEEDBACK...

"A supportive community (professional and personal) is vital. Twitter is great for sharing high-fives and face-palms with fellow freelancers. In real life, I use a couple of nearby coworking spaces to force myself to change out of my PJs every now and then. I'm also lucky to have a few close friends who have travelled the freelance road."

@sallymfoxwrites

"Working from home is not for me. I need noise and laughs and 'ooh did you see that thing last night on the telly?!'. I work in a shared studio space with other creative freelancers. It doesn't just make me more productive and focused; it means there's a proper break between work life and home life, too."

@TurnerInk

"I go to my local coworking space at least once a week. It helps me focus when I've got a major case of procrastination at home. There are fewer distractions, and other people's concentration rubs off on me. Oh, and the coffee is good!"

@fierce_content

"Lean on your community. The amount of times I've fallen back on the freelance community in dark times and had those guys come through for me is shocking. I even had a total meltdown to a fellow writer in my Twitter DMs once and had that person calmly and kindly coach me through it.

"The other thing that works for me is sharing a workspace. Making time to work in public can have a really positive effect on your mental health. Get yourself to a library, a coffee shop, or find a coworking space that suits you – even when you really don't feel like it. You'll feel better for it."

Emma Cownley, copywriter and blogger

"I plan on joining a coworking space later this year as I'm going crazy working from home! I've suffered from depression and anxiety for years and being alone all the time has exacerbated the issues. I find the lack of daily contact impacts my willingness to leave the house for other things and it's turned me into a hermit. Not only has working alone proved to be bad for my mental health – it's had a negative effect on my physical health, too. I've been diagnosed with type 2 diabetes because I sit at home all day and don't exercise."

@TheContentType

"Investing in a private office within a coworking space was the best thing I ever did. It provides a sense of community, adds structure to my working day and makes me more productive. I've made friends with other freelancers, and it's great to have people to bounce ideas off and to practise languages together."

@LawyerLinguist

"I've just started my 24th year freelance. Probably the worst thing is the lack of colleagues. Okay, there were some who deserved to be worked over in a dark alley (only kidding) but there were lots of people it was great to work with. I get around this by networking; it may bring in business but the real reason I do it is to mingle with people who aren't clients."

Phil Chambers, safety consultant

"I was considering using a coworking space until I worked from someone's office for a week while my neighbours were having work done. I was surprised to find how much I disliked it. I couldn't talk to myself or exercise while using the 'read aloud' function. I also detested the shared microwave and toilet situation! I'm currently reading *Company Of One* which is making me feel better about my antisocial working preferences!"

@LauraLSands

"I never went into this thinking it would be easy – far from it – but it's tough. There's so much I didn't prepare myself for! I've found the online freelance community helps beyond anything. Having people talk about and share their experiences openly and honestly means you're never alone. There's always someone to help you rise back up, and steady you while you do so. I'm thankful to have a crew of exceptionally amazing, caring and kind people holding my hand."

Maxine Kerley, digital marketing strategist

"A couple of years ago I was feeling really low about being freelance. Shifts came and went, but I was unfulfilled, isolated and unhappy. I came up with the idea of doing a podcast to connect people who felt the same, so I joined a couple of Facebook groups for podcasters and got started. Now I get feedback from other freelancers telling me they find it a lifeline!

"Freelance Feels started as a little idea; I never dreamed it'd become what I wanted to do for my main business! So, don't be afraid to lean on the freelance community. There's safety in numbers!"

Jenny Stallard, lifestyle journalist and founder of freelancefeels.com

"Before going freelance, I had a work-from-home job. While it was an absolute novelty at first, it became very lonely and isolating after just a few months – especially as I didn't get out and about much given my type of role. When I went freelance, I told myself I had to join a coworking space – and I love it! It's so much more than just a desk, coffee and wifi – there are opportunities to network, collaborate and mentor, and so much more."

Steve Morgan, SEO expert and author of Anti-Sell

"I find networking with other freelancers to be the most productive in terms of enjoyment and new business leads. The more formal corporate breakfast-type events don't suit me, but I go to a local event for small businesses once a month. I even did a presentation at the last one, about how to get media coverage for your business. I mainly did it to practise giving presentations, but lots of people said they found it helpful."

Mary Whitehouse, copywriter

MYTH TWO

"I have to do it all: sales, marketing, admin, accounts…"

The reality

Doing everything yourself is the fast train to burnout

Ah, the days of employment: where your time, workload, goals, and salary are pretty much decided for you.

Depending on your own experiences of being managed, you may have been drawn to self-employment precisely because you get to manage everything yourself: not just your time and energy but your finances, your development, and your income.

Sounds good, right? At least on the surface.

Because the stark reality that you're responsible for your own success – and that the buck really **does** stop with you – comes with its own pressure. Those deadlines won't let up just because you're having a rough day, after all.

There's an expectation that freelancers need to be their own accountant, do their own admin, troubleshoot their own tech, and be their own life coach. But it's an unhelpful attitude that's more likely to lead to overwhelm and burnout than a happy, healthy freelance life.

Most of us spend hours each week struggling with tasks we don't enjoy and tackling things we know we're not good at – at least in the early days, when the idea of spending our hard-earned cash on paying for help is inconceivable.

It's a sure-fire way to feel drained, disillusioned and fed up, but we do it because we don't know there's an alternative. (Good news: there is!)

Reality bites

We're attracted to self-employment because we want to make money doing more of the things we love. Reality hits when we get to the end of the week and realise we've spent half our time attending meetings, calling clients, writing proposals, sending emails, chasing payments…

Why does no one tell us just how relentless the 'running a business' bit of freelance life can be?!

Being a control freak with a fundamental inability to ask for help in **all** areas of my life, I attempted to do everything myself for the first 15 years of running my business. Not only did I see asking for help as an admission of weakness, but I also believed that if I wanted something done right, I had to do it myself.

And even though I'd built my business around my kids, as they grew from babies to toddlers to teens, I sucked at setting boundaries!

I never took the time to define where work ended and home life began, and though I mainly managed to resist working weekends, I was always in a semi-state of high alert. What if a client needed me and I wasn't there to respond to their email right away?

I had heaps of work, plenty of clients and was earning a good income, yet self-employment wasn't working for me.

I was constantly stressed, worn down, anxious, irritable and depressed. I never had enough time. I couldn't switch off. I wasn't enjoying life, I wasn't much fun to be around, and I was approaching burnout, fast.

It was only when my home needed decorating that the penny dropped.

I realised I had a choice: I could spend a **lot** of time doing a half decent paint job that I'd be semi-satisfied with, or pay a professional decorator to do it perfectly in half the time.

Back then, I was charging £300 a day. The decorator who'd been recommended charged £100 a day.

I didn't love decorating, I wasn't particularly good at it and it didn't make me money.

Then it occurred to me.

I didn't love doing my accounts, my admin, or my IT support, either.

I'd spend longer procrastinating about doing my tax return than it'd take an accountant to do a year's worth of accounts. Suddenly, it was a no brainer.

If I was prepared to pay a professional to paint my house, I could use the time he was saving me to earn more money.

Ditto a professional accountant, virtual assistant, and IT support company.

It's a simple equation:

as much time as possible doing the things that make you money

+

as little time as possible doing the things that don't

=

the secret to freelance success

I made a commitment to ask for help and to set better boundaries, and I haven't looked back since.

Outsourcing the tasks you don't enjoy, you're not skilled at, and which aren't a good use of your time frees you up to focus on the things that really matter – both to you and to your business.

Sure, it's not always easy to let go, but there simply aren't enough hours in the day to do everything yourself. What's more, recognising that you can't do it all isn't a sign of weakness: it's a sign of strength.

Asking for help shows that you value your own mental and physical health. After all, if you're not taking care of yourself and your own needs, how can you expect to fulfil the needs of the people around you – your friends, your family, and your clients?

It's easy to see why experts say delegation is the key to running a successful business. The sooner you realise – and act on – this, the quicker your small business will flourish.

The advice

Don't be afraid to ask for help

Stick your hand up if you enjoy keeping track of your business expenses or doing your annual tax return… thought not. Yet the number of freelancers who spend time and energy doing their own bookkeeping and accounts is extremely high.

The same goes for the routine admin tasks you don't enjoy, the time you spend trying to fix your glitchy software and hardware, or the hours spent proofreading those proposals (you've spent far too long on them to spot your own mistakes, however hard you try).

Yes, hiring an accountant, virtual assistant (VA), IT consultant, or proofreader costs money. But remember that equation! Paying a professional can save you time and effort, as well as the headache and stress of doing the job yourself.

Surrounding yourself with good people who tackle the tasks you don't enjoy while you spend your days doing the thing you love is the secret to enjoying freelance life.

It's a little like having a cheerleading squad supporting your business and contributing to your success. Your virtual team may include:

- **An accountant**
  There to file your annual tax return, guide you through the business expenses that are allowable and those that aren't, and – when your business really takes off – to handle your quarterly VAT returns[1].

- **A virtual assistant (VA)**
  An admin angel who keeps your client records in shape, handles your day-to-day social media posts and creates clever email campaigns.

- **An IT company**
  No need to have a hissy fit because your laptop's playing up, or to waste hours searching for a lost email – just call your IT helpdesk and they'll fix it fast, for the cost of a takeaway each month.

- **A proofreader**
  A safety net to catch the mistakes that mess up your marketing and the slip-ups that spoil your sales campaigns.

What's more, once you've found the people you can rely on, you'll quickly pick up techniques, tools and tips that make the day-to-day business end of freelance life **so** much easier.

The help you need may depend on your business, but the truth remains the same. Asking for help doesn't just make good business sense: it's vital for your wellbeing and the enjoyment you get from self-employment.

Setting boundaries

When it comes to enjoying freelance life and avoiding stress and burnout, setting boundaries – and knowing when to stop – is as vital as asking for help.

We can all relate to how hard it is to switch off, particularly when there's no office to leave behind. And the flexibility of self-employment can be a mixed blessing if it means you never stop thinking about work.

April Doty, herself a freelancer, and part of the Minds@Work[2] team, agrees: "When you become a freelancer, the meaning of work changes: work is no longer a place you go to – it's the output that comes from you.

"Work doesn't start and end when you pass through the front door of the office, so we need clearly defined goals and ways to measure our own progress and achievement.

"Some of us feel the need to prove ourselves, since no one can see how hard we're working. Overworking is common, and unrealistic expectations can create unhealthy pressure that can lead to burnout, anxiety, and depression.

"But what counts as work isn't as simple as it seems. In the old world, 'work value' was synonymous with 'time spent in the office', yet no one sits in front of the computer typing for eight hours without interruption. Instead, we check in with colleagues and talk about last night's football game, eat cake in the kitchen, and have impromptu meetings in the hallway about a new idea or project...

"In spite of these seemingly trivial social distractions, we never question whether we're working enough – we know we're working because we're in the office!

"As freelancers, we must honour the time we spend developing new ideas and building relationships, because without this creativity and collaboration, work would grind to a halt. Now that work is no longer contained to a specific time and place, it's up to us to set boundaries and safeguard our personal time, because full rest and recovery are vital to the thriving mental health that fuels our best performance."

Overworking is common, and the dangers are clear. According to a 2018 study on behalf of the Mental Health Foundation[3], 74% of UK adults have felt overwhelmed or unable to cope at some point.

Setting boundaries around work and home is the only sure-fire way of keeping stress in check, and achieving the elusive work–life balance we all dream of.

---

1 The threshold for VAT registration (April 2020) is £85,000: gov.uk/vat-registration-thresholds

2 Minds@Work is a movement for mental wellbeing in the workplace: mindsatworkmovement.com

3 Stress: are we coping? mentalhealth.org.uk/publications/stress-are-we-coping

Time out...

Take a moment to outline the tasks you do in a typical working day.

Rate each task according to:

- how good you are at it

- how much you enjoy doing it

This is a great way to recognise the routine jobs that zap your time and energy without making you money. Consider outsourcing these tasks so that you can spend more time on the profitable activity you enjoy.

FREELANCER FEEDBACK…

"The advice I give to most of my clients is stop trying to do everything yourself. There's a common belief that we have to wear many hats as a freelancer. Why? Play to your strengths and outsource the rest! People are usually surprised at the affordability."

Matt Essam, creative business coach

"There are three great reasons to outsource the jobs you don't like. First, while it might seem an additional expense, it could actually save you money. If your time is worth more than what you're paying an accountant, VA, or other professional, then you're saving. Secondly, you're avoiding something you don't enjoy and may not be good at. Thirdly, you could be supporting a fellow freelancer, which is always a good thing to do."

Jonathan Pollinger, social media trainer

"I discovered some of this the hard way, but the output of my work, my marketing material and my business message have far greater clarity since working with experts. I strongly recommend outsourcing the tasks you don't enjoy, and that don't make you money."

Emma Courtney, coach and trainer

"One of the joys of running your own business is that you choose the hours you work, the time you spend, and how it fits into everything else that is important to you. Sure, there are times when the midnight oil might be needed, but this should be the exception not the habit. Outsourcing the tasks you don't enjoy is an effective way of creating and respecting your own boundaries, and avoiding overwhelm."

Gill Smith, business mentor and trainer

"Play to your strengths and team up with others who have specialist skills where you don't. Not only will the final output be better, you're also building yourself a little support network."

Matthew Knight, founder, Leapers

"Ask yourself, 'What would a real business do?' Then start treating your freelance career as a real business. It took me a while to get to this point, but now I'm happy to outsource and pay for expert skills that I don't have, and for help with things I don't enjoy doing. I have an assistant, an accountant… in fact, a whole team of people supporting my business."

Nick Parker, copywriter

"People often think taking on new staff is the only way to grow your business, but most freelancers don't want to go down that route. My business reached a point where I couldn't take on new clients without growing. I wanted to be able to provide a professional service to more clients, but simply didn't have the time.

"My solution was to invest heavily in software partnerships that enable me to automate some aspects of my service. Combining this automation with help from two admin assistants has enabled me to take on more clients, and to automate tasks that would take significantly longer to complete manually."

Chris Attwood-Thomas, SEO consultant

"To be successful as a freelancer, you need to pay other people to do things for you when it makes sense to do so. Trying to do everything yourself ends up being a false economy."

Joel Hughes, WordPress consultant

MYTH THREE

"I'm just a freelancer. It's not the same as running a business!"

The reality

You won't succeed until you take your business seriously

The fact that you're reading this book shows you're committed to making a success of self-employment – yet too many freelancers don't take their work seriously.

They see the word 'freelance' as a casual way to describe someone who's hired for their time and skills – one rung down the career ladder from the business owner or consultant and perhaps even a little… disposable.

I have news for you: it's all semantics.

It's not enough to take a half-hearted approach to your career if you want to make a success of freelance life. As you're reading this book, I'm confident you know this.

Clients and colleagues won't take your business seriously until you do the same – and the sooner you adopt the mindset, procedures, and approach of a business owner, the sooner you'll succeed.

Start by...

- setting yourself up as a business (because you are)

- treating your finances as if you were a business (because you are)

- scheduling your working days as if you were running a business (because you are)

- taking your finances seriously, as if you were running a business (because you are)

- talking about your work as a business (because – surprise! – it is)

Whether you realise it or not, you're running a business. A teeny tiny business, maybe, but a business all the same. And it's vital that you understand this.

When I started my business, back in 1999, the internet was pretty scarce, social media didn't exist, and the idea of a freelancer having their own website was more unusual than snow in July.

I was working part-time hours spread over just three days a week, but that didn't matter. To me, the word freelancer had no negative connotations. I took my business seriously from day one and I made sure everyone around me did the same. (Yes, I'm working from home, and no, you can't just pop by for coffee.)

Hell – I had real experience of working in real businesses with real clients who had real budgets and real deadlines! I didn't want to attract clients with rubbishy, low-paid, unfulfilling jobs – most of whom didn't value their own businesses, let alone mine!

I knew it wouldn't be easy, but I knew how business worked. If I wanted to attract half-decent clients with half-decent budgets, I needed more than a half-arsed approach.

I had branded business cards, compliment slips and letterhead printed ready for my very first day as a freelancer and invested in my first website just three years later.

I finally had a need for the office furniture catalogues that had been dropping through my letterbox with efficient regularity! I chose a corner desk and a comfortable chair, and set up an office in my spare bedroom.

I bought a Mac laptop, a cheap inkjet printer, and an unfeasibly large scanner. I purchased highlighters and red pens in unnecessarily large quantities, and built spreadsheets to keep track of my finances.

I was investing in my fledgling business – both financially and emotionally – and I was ready to go.

Day one, and with my red pens lined up on my desk and my in-tray well and truly empty, I set about tackling the hideously cringeworthy task of sending cold enquiries to people I didn't know.

I had a few contacts I'd built up and nurtured during my time in employment, but really and truly? I was pretty much on my own from the start.

Like any scattergun approach, many of my cold enquiries fell on deaf ears. But d'you know what? Because I'd stepped into the head space of 'a proper businessperson' that's exactly how I was treated by everyone who **did** respond.

When you invest in your career and adopt a business mindset, you'll be amazed at the results.

The advice

Adopt the right mindset
and invest for success

If you want to succeed as a freelancer, you need to get serious about your business. As well as adopting the right mindset, this means investing in your business. But what might you need to invest **in**?

Here are some ideas to get you started:

1. *Technology, tools and equipment*

2. *Your brand*

3. *Your online presence*

4. *A professional website*

1. *Technology, tools and equipment*

Whatever job you do and whatever field you work in, you need up-to-date, reliable tools and technology to do your job properly.

If you're using an ancient version of Microsoft Word that crashes every five minutes, a printer that jams so often you're tempted to chuck it through the nearest window, or a works van that won't get you to the job on time, you can't do your best work.

If you're not doing your best work, you're not providing your clients with a professional service. And if you're not providing a professional service, you won't get the repeat work, referrals, and recommendations that are vital when it comes to establishing your business.

Depending on the job you do, your essential tools are most likely to include a laptop or desktop computer, printer, mobile phone and other hardware. You may also need software, apps and subscriptions to cloud-based accounting software such as QuickBooks, Xero or FreeAgent.

2. *Your brand*

If you want to attract high-value clients who appreciate your skills and experience – and who have the budget to pay you a decent fee – you need to look the part.

This is where your brand comes in.

As a solo worker you may want to compete with larger businesses or agencies – great! But even if you don't plan on playing with the big kids, you'll need a professional image that reflects who you are, what you do, and why you do it.

The same applies whether it's day one of your freelance journey, or you're ten years into self-employment.

To many business owners, the word 'brand' is synonymous with 'logo', but your brand is so much more than that.

Your brand incorporates:

- your business name

- your colour scheme

- typography and fonts

- business cards and stationery

- the way you write about your business (your tone of voice)

- your domain name

- your website

- your email address

- marketing materials such as brochures, flyers and postcards

- your emails and email signature

- your social media posts and profiles

... and it needs to be clear and consistent, wherever your customers see you.

Your freelance brand should be completely authentic to you. Trying to be something you're not is exhausting. Don't go for a slick, polished brand if you're not a slick, polished person or choose a casual, chatty tone if you're more formal and reserved.

Some business owners – particularly in the trades – go as far as wearing branded clothing such as T-shirts and fleeces, while others coordinate their outfit and accessories with their corporate colours when attending networking events and meetings.

Whether you choose to take your personal brand to this level or not, showing that you take your business seriously makes it easier for clients, customers, and colleagues to do the same.

3. *Your online presence*

One thing that far too many freelancers overlook is the need for a professional email address. Your email campaigns are a lot less likely to be taken seriously if they come from fluffyjojo@hotmail. com, so get this sorted before you launch your business.

How? The first step in getting a professional email and website address is to secure a domain name for your business. This is a vital business asset, so it's nice to be in control of it. For this reason, I'd recommend handling your domain name registration yourself.

I **didn't** do this.

Way back in 2002, when my first website went live, anything remotely internet-shaped felt to me like some arcane dark art. But help was at hand: I had a good friend who owned a graphic design business. This was his bread and butter, and I trusted him.

We talked about my website, and he offered to secure sarahtownsendeditorial.co.uk for me. When the time came to make big changes to my site many years later, said friend had done a disappearing act – and you can't begin to imagine the sticky heap of trouble I went through to get my own domain name back!

Rich Bell, director of my current web hosting company, Maple Rock Design, agrees that it's a good idea to secure your domain name yourself.

He goes on to caution against buying email addresses that come packaged up as part of your website hosting. Instead he recommends using a service such as Microsoft Office 365 or G Suite from Google, which has the benefit of keeping your emails separate from your web hosting.

4. *A professional website*

Once you have your domain name secured, it's time to think about a website. As I tell my clients, having a professional website does more than make you stand out and get you found on Google (using the powers of search engine optimisation – often called SEO). A great website puts you in a strong position to compete for projects – and clients – with bigger budgets.

If you have the budget to invest in a website, you'll need:

- a copywriter to help you identify and communicate the things that make your business great

- a web designer to create an eye-catching design that reflects who you are, and the services you offer (based on your brand)

- a web developer to build the site, and to make sure everything works as it should

- a photographer or illustrator for the finishing touches

If you don't have the budget, doing it yourself may be your only option. There are plenty of DIY site builders out there – Wix and Squarespace are just two examples.

Of course, there's the issue of whether creating your own website is the best use of your time – let alone whether you have the skills or the inclination to do it! (See **myth two** for more on the importance of hiring a professional.)

Ultimately, the beauty of having your own website is that it can start small and grow with your business over time – just as long as futureproofing is factored in from the start. Sometimes a simple presence is enough to get you started.

The importance of social media

While we're on the subject of your online presence, it's worth mentioning social media. Platforms such as LinkedIn, Twitter and Facebook are a great way to build your freelance brand and raise awareness of the services you offer.

Something that's often overlooked is the role social media plays in online search. Well-written social media profiles – incorporating relevant keywords and phrases – can help boost your chances of being found online.

To put this to the test, type the name of your business into your browser search bar. You should notice that results from the major social media platforms crop up on the first page of search results, together with your own website, if you have one.

(If you're new to the freelance game and haven't yet built up an online presence, you can test this by typing in 'Sarah Townsend Editorial'.)

What's more, unless you decide to invest in advertising or sponsored posts, social media has the added benefit of being **free**.

But, while it can be an affordable way of finding and attracting new clients, social media can also be a gigantic distraction and an enormous source of pressure if you don't keep things in check.

You may feel you should be:

- digging deep and paying to advertise on Facebook

- sharing thought-provoking posts on LinkedIn

- posting daily inspiration on Instagram

- asking clients for recommendations each time you finish a project

- sharing your wittiest inner thoughts and best GIFs on Twitter

- creating aspirational boards on Pinterest

But you shouldn't.

The biggest mistake most freelancers make is trying to maintain an active presence across the full social media spectrum. Instead, it's best to pick a couple of platforms and do them really, really well.

Ultimately, there's no harm in setting up a profile on every platform if you're determined to cover all bases – it certainly won't hurt your Google ranking. But as long as your information is up-to-date and relevant, it's usually enough to maintain a presence and check in regularly to respond to any messages.

The platforms you choose to focus on will depend on the type of business you're running and where your customers are. Business to business (B2B) freelancers may find LinkedIn and Twitter more effective, while those who deal with consumers (B2C) and have tangible products to photograph and share may prefer the more visual platforms such as Instagram and Pinterest.

Do your research and experiment until you discover where your dream clients hang out, then focus your efforts there.

Finding the right tone of voice

Talking about promoting yourself online raises an important question: should you be open about being freelance or hide behind the guise of a larger business?

Good business is about authenticity and openness – and that means being proud of who you are and what you do, rather than pretending to be something you're not.

Sure, there may be circumstances in which appearing to be a bigger company than you really are can be advantageous – such as when you're pitching for a large contract. Even then, there's nothing to stop you collaborating with a team of trusted freelance friends when you need to. It's a great opportunity to build your own network, for starters.

I'm often asked by my sole trader clients if they should use **I** and **me** when they're talking or writing about their business, or whether it's better to pretend to be a bigger operation than they are, and use **we** and **us** – and I almost always recommend the former.

Here are four reasons why small is beautiful in business:

1. *Confidence*

2. *Consistency*

3. *Continuity*

4. *Cost*

Let's look at these in more detail.

1. *Confidence*

Having the courage to stand proud as a freelancer – and both talking and writing about your business using **I** and **me** rather than **we** and **us** – communicates confidence and self-belief. It may not be very British to say you're great at what you do, but if you don't believe it on at least some level, why should your clients?

2. *Consistency*

Your clients and customers know they can expect a consistently high standard of work – delivered by you, and no one else. Chances are this is the reason they hired you in the first place.

3. *Continuity*

Your clients get to develop a relationship with an expert rather than being passed from person to person. We've all experienced the disappointment of being sold to by the business owner, only to find ourselves dealing with an intern or junior member of the team when it comes to delivering the work. It's not the path to excellent service.

4. *Cost*

Small can mean more affordable. It's not always the case, but smaller businesses usually have lower overheads – which often means lower rates.

Steve Folland, founder of Being Freelance, agrees. "Big businesses spend hundreds of thousands on marketing that makes them sound like small businesses because customers are crying out for the personal touch – think of the growing popularity of advertising that uses words like artisan, handcrafted and homecooked.

"As a freelancer, you already have that advantage. We're all individuals, and your personality and individuality are what make you great at what you offer – don't hide them by trying to sound like a big business."

So, play to your strengths as a freelancer – just don't play small.

Clever thinking

If all this talk of investing raises concerns that you simply can't afford to take your business seriously, try thinking creatively. For example, perhaps you're a freelance accountant and you need a great website to help you stand out from the crowd. If you know someone with the talent and the skills you need to create a professional presence, suggest a skill swap. You may get lucky and find they need your services just as much as you need theirs.

Investing in your business is no guarantee of success. After all, purchasing the latest camera, lenses, post-production software and a super-slick website won't help you make it as a videographer if you have zero skills!

But having the skills, the business mindset, **and** the tools for the job gives you the best chance of success – whatever your chosen freelance career.

Time out…

Investment in your business doesn't come cheap, so it helps to prioritise your wish list. Write a list of your 'must-haves' and 'nice-to-haves'.

Include categories such as:

- **marketing** (a professional website, brochure, logo, stationery, brand design and any promotional items you might need)

- **technology, tools and equipment** (laptop or desktop computer, printer, mobile phone and other hardware, software, subscriptions, and apps)

- **clothing** (promotional T-shirts, sweatshirts, or jackets)

- **transport** (works van, company car, or bike)

FREELANCER FEEDBACK...

"I left a corporate job for self-employment nearly 20 years ago. I started with a cheap secondhand van and the most basic tools I could get away with. Over the years I've put money aside to invest in my business, and it's really helped.

"Having a professional image is really important in the trades. When I turn up to quote for a job in a sign-written van, wearing a T-shirt with my business name on, people can tell I'm a professional. It means I'm more likely to get decent work for clients with decent budgets, and the van is a great way of attracting new customers."

Darren Packer, plumber and renovation specialist

"When I started freelancing, someone told me, 'If you want clients to invest in you, you have to invest in you.' Start small: get a website and custom email address, use a consistent photo and branding across social media. It all builds credibility and shows you're serious about your work. I didn't spend a fortune (free WordPress template, Canva images, secondhand desk and chair...) but it really helped me feel professional. And as my clients got bigger, I kept on investing."

Amy Boylan, copywriter

"The sooner you start taking your figures seriously and act like a business, which exists to make a profit – with systems and processes, a professional website, brand, email signature and email address – the sooner you'll succeed as a freelancer."

Steve Folland, founder, Being Freelance

"If you're not operating as a freelancer with a 'business' mindset, there's a danger that you will end up working too many hours, for too little money and your clients will feel like bosses. When you adopt a business mindset, you can position yourself as an expert in your field, you can set your own prices, based on your talent, experience and results – and your clients will respect and value you more than ever."

Louise Jenner, The Dream Job Coach

"I've always taken my business seriously. It would be impossible to secure the high-budget, high-end clients I work with if I wasn't entirely professional, as well as passionate about what I do.

"I set up my business just two years ago, and I'm already in the fortunate position of being too busy to take on new clients. One thing that helped a lot was choosing the right business name, and I think that's often overlooked. Cotswold Buying Agent ranks highly online as well as summing up who I am and what I do. I've also taught myself to use QuickBooks for my accounts, which has helped to streamline the process of invoicing."

Samantha Scott-White, property search agent

"I have a graphic designer friend who needed a piece of writing done to a high standard. I needed a quick logo and business cards designed. Sometimes the barter system works best if you know other creative types."

Fraser McFarlane, creative copywriter

"I invested in a sign-written van when I set up my business. I know other decorators who rock up to jobs in their car with their kit loaded in the back but having a nice works vehicle looks much more professional.

"I buy a stock of branded T-shirts and hoodies once a year to help me stand out – plus it means I'm not getting my own clothes covered in paint! It's not particularly expensive either: a branded polo shirt costs me around £10. As for marketing my business, I pay for an ad in a local magazine to get my name out there, and I'm just getting started with a Facebook page so I can share photos of my work."

Toby Webb, painter and decorator

MYTH FOUR

"I'm still building my reputation. It's okay to work for free sometimes."

The reality

If you don't value yourself, your clients won't, either

Being unsure of how much to charge when you start freelance life is one of the most daunting things about going it alone. It's also one of the most common concerns.

But the chances are that even the more experienced freelancers among you have the occasional wobble – if not an ongoing feeling of anxiety – when it comes to charging.

You agonise over what level to pitch your prices at, fearing being judged for being too expensive ("who does she think she is?") or too cheap ("he can't be that good").

You dread conversations about money and wouldn't dream of asking your new client what their budget is for fear of causing offence.

You worry that increasing your prices would drive clients away – and you end up charging the same for years as a result.

Eventually, you put a quote together, convince yourself the client will never pay that much, knock a bit off, then end up feeling undervalued and unappreciated when you find yourself working round the clock for a pittance.

The first business book I ever read was *Don't Worry, Make Money,* by Dr Richard Carlson, author of *Don't Sweat the Small Stuff.*

One piece of advice in the book influenced my money mindset and the way I charged for my services from day one.

By the time I went freelance, I already had a chunk of marketing experience under my belt. I didn't want to under-price, but I didn't want to price myself out of work, either.

The book shared a case study of a woman who had run her own business for years. She was constantly busy; never had enough hours in the day, nor a moment to spare – let alone time to work on her business. She was undercharging for her services and was falsely overbooked as a result.

The author told her to increase her rates. As an example, they looked at a worst-case scenario based on doubling her fees and losing half her clients. Sounds pretty scary, right? But if she took their advice, not only would she make the same amount of money in half the time, but the clients who stayed with her would be the ones who could afford her higher fees, and were likely to refer her to contacts who were in the same position.

You may not feel comfortable with doubling your rates (though I know business coaches who would give the same advice) but increasing your prices can be a sound principle. By charging more, you're putting a higher value on your time. You'll have more time to dedicate to your clients and projects, rather than knocking out job after job, and you're more likely to feel a sense of pride and fulfilment in your work.

Freelance isn't free

If there's one thing all freelancers have in common, it's the depressing regularity with which we're asked to work without pay – or, at least, for a lot less pay than we deserve.

I'm all for being generous with your advice. I don't believe you should set your clock and start charging the minute you begin sharing your wisdom. There's a lot to be said about the benefits of helping others, and I'm not a fan of charging for every little thing.

But there's a world of difference between someone asking for a little free advice and expecting you to provide a service for free – however much they try to dress it up with "you'd be doing me a huge favour!" and "it'll only take a minute".

We've all experienced clients who promise you exposure in exchange for services. They come in heavy with the slick sales pitch on how they're going to be huge, they have an audience of thousands, and how working for them will be **so** good for your career.

Then they casually drop in – almost as an afterthought – that they just can't afford your prices right now…

But exposure doesn't pay the bills. And, even if you did accept their measly offer because you're just starting out and desperate to build your portfolio, you'll end up cursing the day you met them.

It's a universal truth that the clients who question costs (or refuse to pay) always – without exception – end up being the biggest pain in the butt.

They'll micromanage every last detail. They'll chase you endlessly (though you've never missed a deadline). And they'll never be satisfied.

Instead of panicking each time someone tells you they can't afford your prices, treat it as a sign that this particular client simply isn't the right fit for your business.

Politely decline their offer, let them step aside, and get ready to welcome the next opportunity that comes your way. One that recognises the value in you, and the services you provide.

So, how **do** you decide what to charge?

The advice

Charge a fair price that reflects your skills and experience

That's easy for me to say. But what does a fair price look like?

Every freelancer is different. We have different experience, different strengths, and different skills. We operate in different industries, where benchmark rates vary dramatically. We have different lifestyles and living expenses, and we need different amounts to live on.

All of these combine to influence what you charge – and I don't have a one-size-fits-all answer. What I **do** have is some tried and tested advice to get you up and running.

Depending on your experience, you may need to be flexible and competitive during the early months when you're still building your business and your reputation, and you don't have a heap of recommendations and referrals to fall back on.

You may be so grateful for the smallest sniff of interest from a potential new client that you've talked yourself into doing the first job that comes along for £2.50 and a Mars Bar before you know it.

But being realistic – even competitive – isn't the same as under-charging. Underpricing can dent your self-esteem, drive down rates for everyone in your trade, and attract the kind of clients who don't value your services. What's more, becoming known for being cheap can harm your reputation in the long run.

So, however tough those early months prove to be, resist the temptation to pitch your rates too low simply to undercut your competitors.

The Goldilocks effect

There are a number of steps you can take to help you decide on a decent and competitive rate that's just right for you.

Not too steep, not too cheap... somewhere comfortably in the middle.

As a freelancer, you don't get sick pay, holiday pay, parental leave, a pension, life assurance or bonuses – and you need to take this into account when you're working out what to charge.

Other things to consider include:

- **Your experience and qualifications**
  If you've spent 10 years in employment doing the job you're now doing as a freelancer you'll want to charge significantly more than someone who's fresh out of college and new to the game.

- **Your location**
  Living expenses in both the country and the area in which you're based can affect what you charge. For example, in the UK, London-based freelancers tend to charge more than those living in rural areas.

- **The market**
  You may face intense competition for work, depending on what industry you work in. Someone with an unusual set of skills, a different approach, or a particular niche may be able to charge more, simply because of the demand for their service.

The danger of day rates

I've never been a fan of day rates, which is why I rarely quote one. If a client's first approach is "Hi, what's your day rate?" it's a sure sign they're looking to buy on price and may not value your services.

Picture the scene. A company wants to hire a freelancer in your line of work. They do a quick online search, ask three freelancers for their day rate, and get three responses: £600, £400, £200.

They hire the freelancer with the cheapest rate.

What the client doesn't know is that their chosen freelancer is new to the game and not particularly confident (hence the rate). They need a lot of handholding throughout the process, take twice – or even three times – as long as the most expensive freelancer to do the work, and deliver a result that's half as good.

That cheap job suddenly looks a lot more expensive.

One of my favourite quotes is: "If you think it's expensive to hire a professional, wait until you hire an amateur." If only more businesses knew that their attempts to cut costs could have such disastrous consequences!

If you're determined to charge a day rate, there's a simple calculation that's often quoted. It involves working out the annual salary you want to earn, adding expenses, and dividing the total by the number of weeks you want to work.

But this over-simplistic calculation should come with a big red warning sign. Because it doesn't account for the fact that a huge proportion of your working week is taken up by unpaid activity. Things like marketing your business, going to meetings, doing your accounts, and building your network of freelance colleagues and potential clients.

What's more, it bases your entire business model around doing paid work five days a week. This isn't just unrealistic: it's a recipe for burnout.

Adding value

The freelance model that represents trading a service for a fee gets a fair amount of criticism. At its simplest, it encourages us to exchange money for time.

A far better approach is to charge a fixed fee that's based on the value of the work you're delivering, and not just the time and effort involved. As well as being a more realistic approach, it has the advantage of enabling the client to budget.

I quote a fixed fee for all copywriting projects. My clients pay a 50% deposit upfront, and the remaining 50% on completion of the first draft. Charging a deposit is a great way to protect yourself. Not only does it ensure you have the client's full commitment, it's also a godsend when it comes to smoothing out that ever-unpredictable cashflow.

Remember, your clients are hiring you because you have skills and talents they lack. What may seem simple and second nature to you won't be so easy – or so obvious – to them. While refining and completing a piece of work may take you just a couple of days, the same work could take them the best part of a month to even begin.

Depending on what industry you work in, you may or may not be able to adapt a value-based charging model. But however you charge, **always** provide a clear description of precisely what is (and isn't) covered by your estimate.

Set this out in a clear proposal document, reinforced by a written contract, and be crystal clear that any changes in the scope of the project will affect your fee. This sounds obvious, but you'd be surprised how many people don't do this and end up having an awkward conversation with the client further down the line.

Overcoming the cringe factor

Speaking of awkward conversations… when you're responsible for your own paycheque, it's vital to get comfortable talking about money.

What's more, you need to have confidence in what you decide to charge. The reason for this might sound a little weird but bear with me.

If, on some level, you don't believe you're worth the rate or the fee you're asking for, your client will sense it. They'll be extremely unlikely to take you up on your offer, and equally likely to haggle or quibble over your cost.

How will they know?

Remember when you were a kid, and your mum busted you for sneaking another cookie when she'd already told you you'd had enough?

Just as the guilt was written all over your face back then, your lack of self-belief will seep out of you. If you're having a face-to-face conversation, your discomfort will reveal itself in micro-gestures of hesitation that ooze out of you in your body language and posture. If you're emailing a quote or proposal, your lack of conviction will leak into your language.

Settling on the right pricing strategy for your business can be a game-changer. Sure, it can take a little trial and error to settle on something that feels just right, but trust your value, learn from your experience, and remember to review your rates regularly.

Time out...

- Start by doing your research. Ask clients, contacts and trusted businesses that you know rely on freelancers how much they pay, and what they base their rates on.

- Talk to other freelancers to get a sense not only of **what** they charge but of **how** they charge. Do they charge an hourly rate or a day rate? Do they quote a fixed fee, or charge by the word (copywriters, don't go there!).

- Search for published rate surveys and rate tools you can use as a benchmark. Most industries publish rate surveys as a guideline, and communities such as Freelancing Females have their own rate tools (see **references** for details).

- To help you get comfortable talking about money, practice saying your rates and prices aloud until it feels more natural. Consider roping in your partner or a trusted friend to roleplay money conversations until they feel comfortable.

FREELANCER FEEDBACK...

"Charging your worth isn't as simple as sticking a zero on the end of a quote. If only! It needs logic and emotion. Because it's not what you have to do to add that zero. It's who you need to be. Use tools to help you logically work out what you need to earn to survive. Build great relationships. And then apply positive mindset techniques to begin to thrive. It's a winning approach that sets you up for success."

Helen Dibble, founder of Incredibble and
author of Feel-Good Fees

"If you're feeling unconfident about a number and not delivering your fee with confidence, write the number down and stick it on your desk where you can see it every day. This strategy was recommended to me, and I've found it really helps!"

Penny Brazier, copywriter

"When you charge per hour, you get cheapskates questioning what you spend every minute on and telling you how quickly things should be done, meaning work gets rushed and your skills undervalued. Consider charging per project and give yourself more time."

@thatcontentshed

"Most of my headache comes from taking on clients who want bottom basement prices but penthouse copy. I'm getting much better, but it's great to have a reminder."

Eva Hatzenbihler, direct response copywriter

"Charging enough can be a struggle when you go freelance, and pricing appropriately is a challenge for most freelancers. Too many people expect you to be happy to do the work for next to nothing. I did too much work for too little in my early days. It's still the thing I struggle with the most, but I feel like I'm getting closer to where I should be."

@LauraLSands

"It's vital to know the value you're providing – and consistently keep delivering it – if you want to make it as a freelancer."

@karolstefan

"If you want someone to do something, it's because you know they have a skill you want. So pay for it. You wouldn't tell a plumber fixing your tap will give them 'exposure' as you'll mention how great they are to your friends.

"My work is not a hobby. My books are not free to me. My education, training and years of experience were not free to me. Giving my time and work away won't pay my bills. Know your worth and stop agreeing to work for free when you know you should be receiving a fee for your skills."

Jane Duffus, writer and speaker

"When I'm feeling nervous about costing something, I channel every client who ever confidently quoted me for a project."

Sarah Symonds, copywriter

MYTH FIVE

"I shouldn't turn work down – even if my instinct tells me to say no."

The reality

If something feels wrong, it probably is

Much of the enjoyment you get from your freelance career comes from finding the clients who are a good fit with both you and your business.

These people make your working life **so** much better.

You look forward to their calls, and leave meetings feeling energised.

Their values and approach resonate with yours: you're singing from the same hymn sheet **and** on the same page.

In a nutshell, you're excited about the prospect of working with them, and you just **know** it's going to be a fruitful and satisfying working relationship.

Conversely, you know on some subconscious level when someone **isn't** the right fit for you.

It starts with a hunch.

Your heart sinks momentarily when their name pops up on your phone, and you end the call with an uncomfortable sense that something isn't quite right.

If you had to articulate what you feel, you probably couldn't. But there's usually a good reason it exists.

Perhaps their business goals are out of sync with your values. Maybe their attitude doesn't sit well with you, they don't value your time or your skills, or perhaps you just don't feel comfortable with what they're asking you to do.

You may come across clients who undervalue your skills, telling you "it'll only take a couple of hours" (you'll be the judge of that). Perhaps they tell you they'd do the work themselves, if only they had time (always a red flag).

The trick is to get really good at listening to the uncomfortable feeling you can't define, and to learn to say no when you recognise it.

I know from my own experience that it can be hard to say no – particularly early on in your freelance journey. It's natural to end up agreeing to everything in those first few months when you want to fill your diary and reassure yourself that going it alone was the right decision.

Money is tight, paying clients are scarce, and you're trying hard to build up your reputation. It feels like your response to any work that comes your way should be an unashamedly eager YES.

So, when is it okay to turn work down?

Accepting projects to build your portfolio and get the money rolling in is a sound way to get you on the path to success. No work means no money – and with mouths to feed and bills to pay, the thought of turning work down brings you out in a cold sweat.

There's no doubt that saying no to projects in these early days seems counterintuitive at best, and plain stupid at worst.

But the time will come when trusting your gut and turning work down is second nature.

Regrets? I've had a few...

You'll work with clients who prove to be so difficult that you wish you'd never met them, and you'll almost certainly accept projects that go off the rails so badly that you end up cursing the desperate day you took them on.

To a certain degree, the difficult clients and punishing projects are an important part of your freelance growth.

Much like the process of dating, these bad experiences help you to identify and refine the type of relationship you **don't** want, so you can spot the warning signs next time around and graciously decline.

It's all part of the process. And, as long as no one is harmed in any way, you can chalk it up to experience.

Those days are gone

In time, you'll build up a steady supply of work from a growing bank of clients. Once cashflow is no longer a dirty word, and the thought of your overdraft no longer brings you out in a rash, you're ready…

It's time to learn to nurture and trust your instinct – and to learn the important and empowering art of saying no.

Sometimes we say yes because we're driven by fear. What if we turn down this work that's being offered to us and nothing comes along in its place? It's a common concern.

The expression "one door closes, another door opens" has been attributed to the scientist, engineer, and inventor of the telephone, Alexander Graham Bell. Like many entrepreneurs, he failed in countless endeavours, only to learn from his mistakes and achieve greater things.

The full quote emphasises the need to focus on the future, "When one door closes, another opens; but we often look so long and so regretfully upon the closed door that we do not see the one which has opened for us."

While spotting the new opportunities may prove hard, try not to make decisions based on fear. Instead, learn to listen to – and act on – your instinct, and stay alert to the breaks and chances that follow.

HOW IS IT FOR YOU?

Graeme Piper, who began his freelance journey in 2016, agrees that it's vital to learn to say no. "When my freelance career was less than a year old, I was still actively building up my client list, portfolio, and bank balance. So, it was a confidence boost when an agency I'd worked with recommended me to a web designer who was looking for a copywriter.

"After a two-hour meeting with the web designer, I was still none the wiser as to what he or his client actually wanted. I was asking the right questions but getting the wrong answers – vague soundbites, stock buzzwords and waffle, but no real brief. I found myself writing web copy with no direction, for a business I had no insight into, and an end client I'd had no contact with.

"When I finally sent the copy to the end client, he didn't like what I'd done. He took weeks to come back to me with amendments and was rude and dismissive in the process.

"To cap it off, it became painfully clear I'd woefully undercharged for the privilege. As the project dragged on, I reached the point where I'd have gladly written the whole thing off and chalked it up to experience."

Trust your instinct

While Graeme liked the agency client, he knew from the start that the project neither sounded, nor felt, quite right. The meeting roused his suspicions on the potential issues that lay ahead, and he now recognises that this should have been the end of that particular collaboration.

Graeme took the job because he couldn't afford to turn work down. But in doing so, he heaped a lot of unnecessary frustration and stress on himself – all because he didn't trust the gut instinct that was telling him to say "thanks, but no thanks".

Wherever you are in your freelance career, cultivating the art of saying no doesn't just save you from headaches and worry: it frees you up to work on projects that excite and fulfil you. Let's look at how we do it.

The advice

Tune in to your instinct, and don't be afraid to say no

Being stuck in a cycle of attracting and accepting the wrong work takes the joy out of freelance life.

Perhaps you're unhappy because the projects that take up most of your working week don't suit the direction in which you want your business to go. Maybe you're caught up with a bunch of small, fiddly jobs when you long for something more substantial. Or perhaps you're the opposite and see the more long-term projects as time-consuming and dull.

Whatever scenario you identify with, spending your precious time and energy on work you don't want prevents you from attracting the work you do.

And because you have neither headspace nor attention to spare, you miss the sliding-doors moments, the chance meetings, and the serendipitous openings that can lead to better opportunities.

Ultimately, the freelance dream is to spend your days working on projects that fulfil you – or, to borrow a phrase from Marie Kondo, that spark joy[1]. Ask yourself, does this job deliver the good stuff?

- **Good times**
  You enjoy working with the client or team involved.

- **Good brief**
  The client is clear on what they want from you, and provides a defined scope of work.

- **Good payers**
  Not only does the client respect you enough to pay a decent fee for your work, but they pay your invoices on time.

- **Good fit**
  The work complements the niche you want to focus on, or the direction in which you'd like your freelance career to go.

- **Good vibes**
  The client's mission and goals are in line with your values.

Starting small

Like most things in life, saying no becomes easier and more comfortable with practice. It can help to start by turning down a couple of small jobs that don't feel right, or which don't fit the framework above.

You know in your heart of hearts that a high-profile, big-bucks project is too much to take on, and that a workload that huge will sabotage your work–life balance. Unless you can collaborate with a team of trusted freelance colleagues, **it's okay to say no**.

Your first contact with a prospective client was fraught with challenges. Your communication practically crackled with conflict, misunderstandings were rife, and you felt like you were at a disadvantage from the off. **It's okay to say no**.

You're already busy and stressed out when you're contacted by a client who wants you to take on a job that simply has to be done this week. **It's okay to say no**.

Above all else, if your instinct is screaming at you to stay away, listen to it.

Of course, there may be occasions when your first assessment of a situation proves to be inaccurate. Just as there are times when saying no is the right thing to do, there are others when a little patience and understanding can lead to a strong and supportive working relationship.

It's a little like the time when the annoying kid in the playground on the first day of school ended up becoming your best friend.

From a business perspective, misunderstandings can arise when a prospective client doesn't appreciate the way you work, the value you can deliver, or the input you need to do your job properly. Sometimes these slow-burn relationships can become rewarding and fulfilling when you invest a little patience and guidance.

Refining your offering

By being selective about the work you take on – and spending more of your time and energy on projects that bring you joy – you'll gradually refine your offer.

You'll become more comfortable talking about the work that truly excites you, the sectors that fuel your fire, and the direction in which you want your business to go.

In turn, this will help you to attract more of the projects you want – those that are more challenging, more rewarding, and better in line with your business goals.

So, listen to your gut and learn to value yourself enough to accept and welcome the work you deserve and to set boundaries that help you say no – both politely and firmly – to the jobs you don't want.

Passing work on

Fit and intuition aren't the only triggers to saying no: you'll also need to turn work down when you're fully booked. If you haven't already experienced this scenario, trust me – the time will come when you simply don't have time to fit in another project, or to take on yet another client, without sending your stress level skywards and jeopardising your own mental health.

If your concerns around saying no relate to letting your client down, consider partnering with a trusted colleague who has similar experience and a comparable approach.

You may be happy to work on a mutual referral basis – where you help one another out by sharing work – or you may prefer to agree a suitable finder's fee. Either way, you can soften the blow of your refusal by suggesting the client discusses the work with your colleague, and introducing them through a simple email.

You've solved the problem for the client, helped your colleague by making a new connection and topping up their sales pipeline, and potentially earned a small referral fee in the process.

This approach taps into the principle of reciprocity, a concept that's covered in Robert Cialdini's book *Influence: The Psychology of Persuasion*.

In a nutshell, when someone does you a favour, your brain is hard-wired to respond in a similar way. So, you introduce a client to your colleague when you're busy; they introduce a client to you when they're busy. You recommend a freelance friend for a project; they recommend you in return.

Sometimes a concise and confident email is the simplest way to say no. "Thanks for thinking of me. I don't have the capacity to take on this work right now, but I can recommend a trusted colleague who may be able to help."

Another approach is to subcontract to another freelancer. This can work, but a word of warning. The client has contacted you because they know, like and trust you. They've picked you because of your reputation, which you've worked hard to build.

If you don't have time to take work on but have a trusted freelance friend you could subcontract to, be honest. Explain your position, give the client the option, and let them decide whether or not to take the risk.

Saying no becomes easier with practice, and having a clear idea of how you want your business to develop can help you to identify the projects – and the clients – to turn down. The exercise in the **Time out...** box that follows will help with this.

---

1   Marie Kondo is the author of *Spark Joy: An Illustrated Guide to the Japanese Art of Tidying.*

Time out...

What's your response when someone asks you why you do what you do? Your initial thought may be "To earn money", but money is a means to an end, not an end goal.

Spend some time thinking about your purpose – the thing that drives you, and the reason you get out of bed in the mornings.

Perhaps you work so you can provide financial security for your family. Maybe you dream of sending your children to university. Perhaps you want to invest in a hobby so you can make the most of your leisure time. Or perhaps you want to raise awareness of an issue that's important to you.

Keeping your purpose in mind can help you make the right business decisions: from the clients you work with to the messages and channels you use to raise awareness of what you do and who you do it for.

Start With Why and *Find Your Why* by Simon Sinek both contain more information on identifying and refining your purpose (see **references**).

FREELANCER FEEDBACK...

"If your gut's telling you that a client or project isn't a good fit or isn't setting you up for success, trust it."

@nelkencreative

"Learning to trust your instinct is vital. I used to say 'yes' to all client approaches when I first became self-employed – I got myself into some right old pickles! Now I trust my instincts. I've turned work down just because I get a bad feeling or don't like the potential client in the first meeting or phone call. Another nicer client usually comes along soon after."

Christian Tait, graphic designer

"Just because someone else is further along their freelance journey doesn't mean you should be. That's their path – your path is yours. So, take your time, and don't compare yourself or your journey with others. Remember, it's not a race. And trust your intuition. If something isn't right for you, your gut will say."

@sjbwrites

"Trust your instinct. Not every job is worth taking – even if you need the money. If you get a bad feeling at the beginning of a project or a working relationship, you'll feel worse at the end."

Deborah Brody, marketing writer and copy editor

"Learn when to say no and when to sack a client. When the money is too little or stress too high, walk away."

@writeything

"Learn to say no. Sometimes we say yes to things that aren't right for us because it feels like our only chance. Then, later down the line, when the thing we said yes to is eating up our time and energy, stress levels rise, and we become overwhelmed. Know your boundaries and stick to them."

@KickstartSophie

"Listening to your instinct is critical, and ignoring it can lead to stress, anxiety and bad professional relationships. If you're second guessing yourself, lean on your community to discuss your concerns and get some objective advice – even the act of writing it out can help, as you see the situation in words, rather than thoughts spinning around in your head."

Matthew Knight, founder, Leapers

"Freelance success requires discipline, motivation, the self-awareness to know when to push vs when to say 'enough' and take a break, and the self-confidence to say 'no'. Finding someone you trust who will call you out when necessary can help."

@jonpearse

"Do you admire small business people who seem to get a lot done? Don't make the mistake of thinking it's due to willpower. Most of the time these folks are acting on a pull rather than a push. It's their vision, passion, or aspiration that keeps them moving."

CJ Hayden, author, Get Clients Now!

"One of my clients asked me to write a series of scripts for a client video he was shooting. Questioning revealed that his client was setting up a new cryptocurrency exchange and the videos were designed to explain the concept. Both the dubious reputation of cryptocurrencies and the fact that the end client was based overseas rang alarm bells for me, but I reluctantly agreed to take on the work to help my client.

"Luckily, I didn't completely ignore my instinct and insisted on being paid a 25% deposit in advance. Unfortunately, my initial instincts proved correct. The cryptocurrency entrepreneur didn't pay my client, and I had to fight to recover the three remaining days of my fee. Next time, I'll trust my instinct and say no!"

Melanie Silver, writer

MYTH SIX

"Freelancing is an easy life.

The reality

Be prepared for hard work

Fair warning: this chapter is a little more personal. I make no apology for this. Money is a very personal matter. We all have our stories, our triggers, and our deep-set beliefs around the issue – and if you can learn from my experience, then the tough stuff is worthwhile.

Uncertainty. Lean times. Highs and lows. Peaks and troughs.

Whatever you call it, the unpredictability of self-employment can be relentless, however experienced you are.

And, while the dream for any freelance career is to reach a point where you can pick and choose the jobs you take on, this takes time and hard graft.

Building your contacts, nurturing your relationships, and establishing your reputation require grit, determination, effort… and a healthy respect for money.

My early experience

I grew up in a family where money was tight. My toys were handmade, and my clothes were hand-me-downs. We didn't have a car, and holidays involved house-sitting for my grandparents' friends while they were away.

My mum gave up her job when she married my dad as they planned to start a family right away. She was a qualified children's librarian; he was an instrument maker in the RAF.

Dad's wasn't a well-paid job – Mum remembers them surviving on £17 a week, which wasn't easy with two growing girls – but it was steady enough, and he enjoyed it.

I was 13 when the US took over the airbase where Dad worked, and he was made redundant. He began applying for jobs right away and received letter after letter telling him he'd been unsuccessful. At the few interviews he got, the feedback was always the same: "You're too old." He was 43.

After a year of surviving on dole money, and with Dad's self-esteem in bits, my parents decided enough was enough. Having made most of the toys my sister and I played with when we were growing up, they began making wooden badges and dolls house miniatures, and selling them everywhere they could.

Though they loved the creativity of the job, they knew nothing about running a business – and this was years before email, the internet and eBay! All they knew was hard work.

It wasn't easy, but they were prepared to put in the time, hard graft and commitment that self-employment demands, and they survived. Eventually, they turned their hobby into their full-time business and became collectable toy dealers – a job that provided them with a modest income for over 30 years.

The importance of saving

The good thing about being raised in an environment where every penny counts is that you make damn sure you **always** have enough to get by. Money becomes your security, and not having enough creates an ongoing anxiety that can lead to a permanent feeling of being off-balance (quite literally).

The bad thing is that if you're not careful, it's easy to become completely neurotic about money… and I **was** completely neurotic about money.

Going solo carries its own share of financial challenges – even when you're charging a decent rate. Every freelancer I know would rather drag themselves into work with pneumonia, toothache and a loose limb than take a day off sick and not get paid. I was no different.

And then there were the holidays. I've talked about boundaries, and how vital it is to take time out to recharge when you're self-employed. I've also admitted it took me years of intense stress and frequent burnout to do anything about it.

I'm ashamed to admit that I struggled for years to justify taking time off for holidays. I would do the maths in my head: five days off at X per day = Y, plus the cost of the holiday. Man, that's one expensive vacation!

From the moment I set my out of office response and shut the door of my spare-bedroom office, the sense of this 'lost income' would loom like a heavy weight over me.

While I was supposed to be enjoying precious family time away from the office, my brain would be working overtime. I'd somehow subconsciously divide the cost of the trip **plus** the money I could've been earning by the number of days we were away, then try to squeeze that much fun out of each and every day.

With all that pressure riding on the holiday, how could I ever relax and enjoy myself? The honest answer is, I couldn't. It put enormous strain on my relationships, not least with my then-husband.

It took me years to stop thinking in these terms, and the change only came with earning what I considered to be 'enough' to realise the value of my leisure time – and the need to relax and enjoy my evenings, weekends and holidays with the people I love.

Looking back, I massively regret those times, but it's hard to identify with the fear of having no money – and the insecurity it represents – if you haven't lived through it.

Let's see how you can learn from my experience.

The advice

Value your time off, and
pay yourself first

When it comes to your wellbeing and mental health, the importance of taking time out can't be emphasised enough. And I'm not just speaking from experience.

Research from the Association of Independent Professionals and the Self-Employed (IPSE) found that taking time off has a substantial positive impact on the wellbeing of freelancers.

According to their 2019 report[1], the vast majority of respondents (92%) said taking time off has at least some positive effect. More than two in five (44%) say it helps them to feel less stressed and anxious, and 59% believe it improves their work-life balance.

IPSE's research also showed that 63% of freelancers believe holidays improve their work performance, and 33% feel more productive as a result.

Yes, freelance life can be hard work but it's vital that you don't let your health and your relationships suffer because of it. Make a commitment to take time off, and to prioritise both your mental and physical wellbeing (see the ideas in **myth seven**). You'll be a lot happier for it.

Money matters

As well as learning to set boundaries and take time out, there are some big financial issues that affect all freelancers. Arguably the most important of these is savings.

It's vital to have a pot of savings behind you before you start self-employment. Most guidance recommends aiming for at least three months of living costs, but the more you have, the better.

Your freelance fund won't just help you survive while you build up your client bank and begin to get paid, though that's a big part of it. It will also enable you to invest in the tools you need for a successful freelance career – such as your website, brand, marketing materials and equipment – all of which are covered in **myth three**.

Cashflow can be a real problem when you're self-employed. Even if you're lucky, you should allow at least a month to secure your first job, a month to complete it and invoice, and another month to get paid[2].

From the money story I've just shared, you won't be surprised to learn that I'm a saver at heart. Ever since I got my very first paycheque, I've saved at least 25% of everything I earn. (I was 16 and working part-time in Woolworths while studying for my A Levels.)

If you have the discipline to start saving while you're still employed, happy days. But getting into the habit of saving at least 25% of each and every invoice is vital when you're self-employed.

Don't spend the tax!

It's appropriate that on the day I put the finishing touches to this chapter, I've just logged into my business bank account to pay a five-figure tax bill.

If you take one piece of advice away from this chapter, make it this: **not all the money your clients pay you is yours.**

As soon as you register as self-employed, you become responsible for paying your own tax. Obvious, right?

But there's something that can catch you out if you're not aware of it. Once your annual tax bill is over £1,000 you have to make payments on account[3]. This involves paying half the following year's estimated tax upfront.

Payments on account are due twice a year, to help spread your tax payments, but that first tax bill can come as a nasty surprise if you're not prepared for it.

What's worse, that ominous brown envelope lands just before Christmas, and the first instalment is due for payment on 31 January. Yup – the tightest and most difficult month of the year.

Don't get caught out. If you're just starting your freelance journey, do your research and speak to an accountant for advice if you need to.

According to a 2019 report by the Money and Pensions Service[4], an estimated 11.5 million UK adults have £100 or less in savings. Yet saving is a vital habit to get into when you're self-employed. Having an emergency fund to dip into when you need it really helps to take the pressure off. It also comes in handy should you become ill or injured and find yourself unable to work.

You may not be a habitual saver like me, but if you can get into the habit of paying yourself first, you'll find those brown envelopes from HMRC a lot less sinister.

Insurance and pensions

The subject of insurance and pensions and why you need them could fill its own book.

I'm not an expert, so I won't attempt to do the topic justice here. Suffice to say: life assurance, income protection, serious illness cover, public liability insurance, professional indemnity insurance, a pension…

I have them; you need them. Talk to an independent financial adviser (IFA)[5].

A note about VAT

If you're just starting out and you expect your business to have high set-up charges, you might want to consider registering for VAT. This enables you to claim back at least some of the tax on the cost of your home office, equipment, training and marketing. An accountant can help you decide[6].

1   IPSE report, *Taking time off as a freelancer*, 2019: ipse.co.uk/uploads/assets/
     uploaded/eae5de3f-af75-477a-be1b838127ba7262.pdf

2   According to IPSE, self-employed workers spend an average of 20 days a year
     chasing late payments, and 43% write off at least one unpaid piece of work:
     ipse.co.uk/ipse-news/news-listing/late-payment-scourge-self-
     employed-across-the-uk.html

3   Payment on account: gov.uk/understand-self-assessment-bill/payments-on-
     account

4   Talk Money, Talk Pensions, 2019, The Money and Pensions Service:
     moneyandpensionsservice.org.uk/wp-content/uploads/2019/10/Talk-
     Money-Talk-Pensions-Week-2019-participation-pack-financial-wellbeing.pdf

5   Find an IFA: unbiased.co.uk

6   Different countries have different issues and different legislation to consider. This
     chapter was written with a UK audience in mind and doesn't attempt to cover the
     legislative issues surrounding self-employment. Always do your research.

Time out...

A little forward planning is essential before you take the leap into self-employment, but it's not just the newbie freelancer who needs to keep a close eye on finances. Even if you don't want to delve into detail in a full-on business plan, it's vital to have at least a basic cash flow forecast and budget.

We **all** need to know what goes out of our bank account each month – even if we don't always know what's going in.

Outline every regular monthly bill and expense. These are your **fixed costs**. Then estimate the bills you can't always predict. These are your **variable costs**.

Next, think about any annual expenses, such as car tax or insurance payments. Divide these by 12 and add to your monthly total.

Search online for one of the many free budgeting and cashflow forecasting tools available if you need help with this.

FREELANCER FEEDBACK...

"Start by saving three months' living expenses (mortgage, petrol, food, etc) in the bank, preferably in a separate bank account. It changes everything."

@Mike_Ames_Flair

"Before I set out as a freelancer, I saved over ten grand to get me through my first three months. It was the most I'd ever saved. It helped get me through the lean months when I didn't have much work in the pipeline, and I pretty much burned through the lot before people started paying me.

"Freelancers never talk about how they structure their bank accounts, but it's really important to find out what works for you and stick with it. I now have a business current account, which all expenses go out of and all invoices are paid into. I keep that capped at £15k – enough to run my business for three months – and anything over that is scraped into two savings accounts: one for tax and one for extras. Being in control of your finances, and knowing you have enough to pay your tax bill, is vital."

Nick Parker, copywriter

"Your business lives or dies by how you budget three things: your time, your money, and your powers of concentration. Use these precious and finite resources carefully. Mixing up the hard and boring stuff with the easy and interesting makes your working life a lot more enjoyable; it's one of the great pleasures of being your own boss."

Ben Masters, copywriter

"Make sure you put a third of everything you earn into savings for tax bill time!"

@QCattQ

"Make sure you're charging enough to allow for losing a third of your earnings to tax and another third to admin and expenses. If you can pay your personal bills and still afford to eat with what's left, you're golden. As for HMRC's payment on account… as far as I'm concerned, they should scream about it when you first register as self-employed.

"Getting landed with an 18-month tax bill shouldn't be a surprise, but nobody mentions it until it comes through the door – and few people have that much extra easily at hand."

@bobblebardsley

"I believe everyone, not just the self-employed, should save a portion of their earnings for future use. There's never a 'right time' to put money aside, but if you can get into the habit, it soon becomes second nature. You have to ask yourself whether you can afford NOT to save.

"What if you were to suffer an accident or illness that stops you working? Could you afford to cover basic living expenses? Stop putting off saving as a 'nice-to-do-when-I-can-afford-it'. Get ahead of the game and make it an essential practice – one you can't afford to put off until it's too late."

Natalie Hull, founder, Sockatoos

"Whether you hire an accountant or do your accounts yourself, never become detached from your figures. It's vital that you know the things that make you money and the things that don't – so you can do more of the former and less of the latter."

Steve Folland, founder, Being Freelance

MYTH SEVEN

"I love my job. Every day should be a good day."

The reality

We all have bad days

"Find a job you enjoy doing and you'll never work a day in your life."

That quote has a lot to answer for.

Like any career, your freelance journey will contain good days and bad.

On a good day, you feel positive, confident, motivated, organised, driven, determined… even untouchable.

You smash deadlines with ease and power through your to-do list with superhuman proficiency. Calls and meetings leave you feeling inspired and energised. You love your job – and your life – with a passion.

Then there are the bad days when you feel like you're a failure, and nothing you can do or say will change the way you feel.

You lack confidence, question your ability to make sound decisions, and find it almost impossible to achieve anything productive. You excel at displacement activity, lack focus, and are easily distracted. Negative self-talk gets the better of you, and you make a convincing show of being your own worst enemy.

I can't stress enough that these ups and downs are **completely normal**. The important thing is to recognise that bad days happen to everyone, and to be kind to yourself when you're going through a tough patch.

Even if you follow all the tips in this book – and remember, it's taken me the best part of 20 years to adopt them all, and I still have off days – working on your own can present challenges to both your wellbeing and your mental health.

Freelancing is often positioned as a fix-all for the problems of employment (and unemployment) – but the reality isn't as clear cut.

Leapers asked 500 solo workers about the relationship between their work and their mental health[1]. Around half of those questioned (48%) believe freelancing has improved their mental health, while 46% believe taking the leap into self-employment has had a negative impact on their mental health.

Spotting the warning signs of burnout

Copywriter, Nick Parker, experienced burnout early on in his freelance journey, and now knows how to recognise the warning signs. "I was a year into my business before I felt like I had any sense that I knew what I was doing, and that things were ticking over. Ironically, it was only when I stopped and took stock that

I realised I'd been living on adrenaline and had no reserves left to keep going.

"I'd spent a year living job to job and invoice to invoice. I'd not long lost my mum, and we were living in rented accommodation while our home was being renovated. Nothing was stable in my life."

That lack of stability, which is an inherent part of freelance life, is tough for anyone. For those who suffer from anxiety – or who are at high risk of burnout – it can be particularly challenging.

Nick admits that a history of anxiety had held him back during his 20s, but by the time he reached his 30s, he'd decided he wouldn't let it stop him doing anything.

"What I didn't realise was that it was a little like driving at 100 miles an hour in first gear. I hit a wall when my mum died in 2013 and I ended up on medication. It was a revelation! I'd thought that everyone felt the same – and that anxiety was just part of everyday life."

Going through burnout taught Nick to recognise the warning signs of living on adrenaline and the risks that entails. "I learned to become more self-aware, to carefully guard my time, money and energy, and to trust my own instincts on the balance of those things in my life. Today, if I find myself 'in the grip', I come off Twitter, eat properly, sleep properly, and remind myself that everything is fine."

Stress and burnout can be all too common when you work for yourself. Learn to recognise the signs that you're taking on too much, and take action to protect yourself. Next, we'll look at some strategies to help you prioritise your mental health and wellbeing.

---

1   How are we doing? Leapers research into freelancing and mental health:
    leapers.co/huru/report/

The advice

It's okay not to be okay

Bad days are far from restricted to the self-employed, but they can feel particularly brutal when you're working alone and have no one to offload on.

We've all been there – even the most seemingly together, sorted, and grown-up among us.

They can strike when you least expect them, for no discernible reason, or as a result of stress, overwhelm, or disappointment – perhaps you didn't get a job you particularly wanted, or a client was less than delighted with your work.

Whatever the cause, don't suffer alone. Instead, reach out to colleagues and peers and ask for help. There are plenty of people out there who will happily listen, support, and empathise (see **myth one** for more on the importance of connection).

Perhaps surprisingly, acknowledging your weaknesses can help to build and strengthen your relationships with others. It does this by creating a vulnerability loop. By openly admitting your imperfections, you send a signal to the other person that it's okay to be imperfect. This mutual understanding helps us bond with others by increasing closeness and trust.

Don't compare yourself to others

Compare and despair they say – and for good reason. The more you look at everyone else's remarkable achievements, superstar social profiles, and perfect portfolios, the worse you feel about your own abilities.

Before you know it, you've talked yourself out of reaching for that goal, pitching for that role and sharing your own small successes because you feel you can't compete.

But no one is getting everything right or doing everything better than you – however much it can feel that way. We're all different, with our own ways of doing things, and those inspiring Instagram profiles and picture-perfect Pinterest boards have been carefully curated to present an image. They're not the chaotic, overwhelming, and joyful messiness of life as a freelancer. It's time we got real about the bad days and challenges that are as much part of the territory as the good stuff.

Remember, the people you see as your competition are human, too. Try reaching out – you have more in common than you realise, and you may even end up with a new friend as a result. Celebrate your own achievements and stop worrying about everyone else's.

Be kind to yourself

We've all heard the quote "Work hard and be nice to people" in relation to success. But it's not just other people we need to be nice to.

Too many of us are guilty of being our own worst enemy from time to time, so learn to keep negative self-talk in check.

The things we repeatedly tell ourselves tend to become our reality, so become aware of the language you're using. If you're in the habit of berating yourself when you make a mistake, and you're unforgiving when something doesn't go to plan, make a choice to be kind to **you**.

Try reframing mistakes as learning opportunities. Instead of saying, "You're an idiot! How could you let that happen?!" tell yourself, "Okay, so that didn't work, but I've learnt from the experience. Next time I'll do it differently."

As a golden rule, if you wouldn't say it to a friend, don't say it to yourself.

Keep your head up...

When it comes to keeping your head above water, we all have different coping mechanisms – and it takes time to learn what works for you.

To quote the author Anne Lamott: "Almost everything will work again if you unplug it for a few minutes, including you". Making time in your working day to reboot your brain and body – whatever that looks like to you – can avoid the long-term consequences of burnout.

Below are some tried and tested wellbeing tips that can help you avoid overwhelm and keep stress in check. Simply taking a short break and indulging in a little self-care can do wonders for your emotional resilience, so choose the methods that work for you and build them into your working life.

1. *Meditate*

2. *Exercise*

3. *Listen to music*

4. *Find your flow*

5. *Get out in nature*

6. *Sleep well*

Let's take a look at each of these in turn.

1. *Meditate*

The benefits of meditation have been known for thousands of years, and advocates swear by the mental and physical benefits of the practice. Meditation is just one way to exercise mental muscles. Regular practice is said to calm the mind and to improve sleep quality, focus, and emotional resilience, as well as helping to alleviate stress, depression, and anxiety, and even chronic physical pain[1].

Easy-to-use smartphone apps such as Headspace, Calm, and Stop, Breathe & Think can be a good introduction to basic meditation techniques. Some apps are free; others work on a subscription basis, and some include a free trial to get you started. If you prefer video, check out the many good examples on YouTube.

Simple guided meditation techniques could work for you, or you may prefer to sit at the top of a hill, watch the clouds, and enjoy the peace, quiet, and fresh air – or to watch the waves crash on a pebbly beach. Making mindfulness and meditation a habit can relieve stress and help you switch off from your bursting inbox and growing to-do list.

2. *Exercise*

Even short bursts of exercise release endorphins – powerful, feel-good chemicals that help to ease stress, anxiety, and depression[2]. And there are endless ways to build exercise into your day. For example:

- Go for a run, swim or bike ride.

- Take the dog for a long walk in muddy wellies.

- Dance around your kitchen while you wait for the kettle to boil.

- Challenge a friend to a game of tennis.

- Pump some iron at the gym.

- Take a yoga, tai chi, or spin class.

3. *Listen to music*

Some people can't work with music in the background; others can't work without it. I'm firmly in the latter category. For me, the world is too quiet without a soundtrack, and even if I can't hear music, there's always something playing in my head.

Create a playlist of uplifting music that'll elevate your mood if you're feeling low, or calming musical wallpaper that keeps you focused in the face of challenging deadlines. (Singing at the top of your voice is optional, but it works for me.)

4. *Find your flow*

Take a break to do a crossword or sudoku, mow the lawn, bake a cake, or wash the car. These tasks, and many like them, can help you to achieve flow: a mental state in which you're so absorbed and focused on an activity that nothing else seems to matter.

The concept of flow was identified by psychologist Mihaly Csikszentmihalyi. In his book, *Flow: The Psychology of Optimal Experience*, Csikszentmihalyi explains that when we focus on a task with no distractions, our mind is 'in order'. Achieving a flow state can help to minimise negative mental chatter and restore a sense of clarity and focus to your day.

5. *Get out in nature*

Studies have shown that spending time outdoors has a positive effect on our mood, together with other therapeutic benefits[3].

Starting your day with a short walk outdoors is a simple way of building both daylight and exercise into your routine. As well as providing valuable headspace and thinking time, it has the benefit of kick-starting the production of dopamine and serotonin – the hormones that are responsible for keeping the blues at bay.

The calming sights and sounds of nature have been proven to lower blood pressure and levels of the stress hormone, cortisol, as well as being an effective way to distract your mind from negative thoughts (and hideous deadlines).

If you live in a rural area you're spoilt for choice, but even city-based freelancers can benefit from taking their mid-morning coffee to a local park for a mood-lifting change of scene. According to researchers at King's College London[4], seeing the sky and trees and hearing birdsong are associated with higher levels of mental wellbeing in urban dwellers.

6. Sleep well

Sleep is as important to our health as eating, drinking, and breathing[5]. It gives our bodies time to repair, and it's hard to function – let alone perform at your best – when you're not getting enough.

Poor sleep is a common cause of health problems – from a weakened immune system to anxiety and depression. Switch off your phone and other electronic devices an hour before bed if you can, to allow yourself plenty of time to wind down.

As well as the tips above, being aware of how and when you do your best work – and using this knowledge to plan your day – will help you get more enjoyment from freelance life.

Structuring your day

Having a limited amount of time to tackle your ever-growing to-do list is a common cause of stress and anxiety – not to mention the seemingly endless drains and distractions when you've no boss or team to keep you accountable.

Though it's easy to fall into the trap of thinking you need to be at your desk from morning to night, the way you structure your day and manage your time is down to you – and taking scheduled breaks can help to keep you motivated, energised, and on track.

Essentially, the hours you work as a freelancer don't matter, as long as you get the work done within the client's timeframe and to a standard both they – and you – are happy with. With this in mind, it makes sense to schedule your day around when you're most productive.

You may work best with the pressure of a deadline. Perhaps you hate mornings and find you do your best work in the evenings and late at night. Maybe your day is topped and tailed by the school run, or the need to take an energetic dog out for a long walk. Or perhaps you're at your most productive first thing, so an early start suits you. The key is to work **with** your natural pattern, not against it.

Finding a routine that works for you

My working day has changed a lot since I set up my business 20 years ago. Like many parents, I started my freelance business part-time, in just a few short hours each week, while my children – then toddlers – were at nursery.

As my children grew, my business grew. As any parent will know, September can be a logistical nightmare for anyone settling a child into a new school. Part-time hours and short days can be crippling to employed parents, but, as a freelancer, I was able to accommodate those tricky schedules in my working day.

I used to get my daily dose of fresh air and exercise by walking my children to school and home again. The biggest change came when they started secondary school. Both got the bus to school and back, and the extra hours this freed up took quite some time to adjust to.

Today's working week is very different. I start work around 7.30am and work four long days with a short break for exercise mid-morning to keep me productive and give me a dose of much-needed endorphins.

As I've already mentioned, I regularly work from the bar at my gym, which is a brisk 15-minute walk from my home. Even on days when deadlines and pressure make organised exercise impossible, nothing makes me skip those short bursts of fresh air and thinking time. They improve my productivity, help to shift writers' block and often enable me to solve any problems that are getting in my way.

HOW IS IT FOR YOU?

Louise Goss founded *The Homeworker* in 2019, and quickly found herself working long hours to get everything done. "I started out saying I wouldn't work late, but the hours crept up – and my excuse was always that the children were in bed! I was becoming exhausted, heading towards burnout and, what's more, the quality of my work was suffering."

Louise found that making simple changes to her schedule increased her productivity: "I've shifted my day to make sure I'm in bed by 10pm or 10.30pm. I now get up and start work a lot earlier. Having worked shifts in newsrooms doing breakfast news, I've learned to be productive earlier in the day. Giving myself time to work with my natural pattern has helped me to feel more prepared and ahead of the curve."

Like Louise, fine artist Melanie Cormack-Hicks has rearranged her working week to suit her life, and is much happier as a result. "My Mondays always started late. Having gone to the gym, got back home, and walked the dog, it'd often be midday by the time I started work – which meant I'd begin the week with an overwhelming feeling of anxiety. I never counted marketing, admin, accounts, or preparation as real work, and any time I wasn't actually painting I'd berate myself for not working hard enough.

"After months of guilt, I began to recognise that the early morning exercise and fresh air were making me more productive. Now Monday is a designated planning day to set me up for the week.

And provided I work really hard on Tuesday, Wednesday, and Thursday, I'm often ready to take things easier on a Friday, which is a great way to start the weekend."

Being in charge of your time and your workload is one of the benefits of self-employment, so remember: run your day – don't let your day run you.

1   Meditation and mental health: psychologytoday.com/gb/blog/balanced/201907/
    meditation-and-mental-health

2   Physical activity and mental health: mind.org.uk/information-support/
    tips-for-everyday-living/physical-activity-and-your-mental-health/about-
    physical-activity/#HowCanPhysicalActivityHelpMyMentalHealth

3   The mental health benefits of nature: health.harvard.edu/mind-and-mood/
    sour-mood-getting-you-down-get-back-to-nature

4   The impact of nature on mental wellbeing: academic.oup.com/bioscience/
    article/68/2/134/4791430

5   The importance of sleep: mentalhealth.org.uk/publications/sleep-report

Time out...

Think about the time of day you're most productive. Are you a morning person or a night owl?

- How could you improve your current schedule to use this knowledge to your advantage?

- What do you need in order to improve productivity?

Try out different working routines until you find one that really works for you.

FREELANCER FEEDBACK...

"You hear so much talk, normally in response to people hating on Mondays, saying that if you go it alone and do what you love, every Monday is suddenly amazing. We can all have a bad day, whether it's work related or not. You can find yourself doubting your decision to go solo because you didn't expect the bad days. Being realistic about this is so important."

Russ Jones-Walker, Pilates instructor

"The worst thing you can do on a bad day is bully yourself into working harder or better. If you need to take an afternoon off or a step back, be kind enough to let yourself do it."

Emma Cownley, copywriter

"Take setbacks on the chin. There will be great times, but there will be difficult, quiet, and desperate times. Keep going, surround yourself with good people who'll help you through, keep pitching for work and getting your name out there, and the tide will turn."

@indeliblethink1

"Make your holidays and weekends real breaks. Don't switch on the computer or check your mail on your phone – instead, put your out of office on and do something you really like. Don't allow yourself to feel guilty that you're not at your desk catching up or working forward on something, even if it's admin or volunteer work."

Jenny Zonneveld, translator

"Figure out what your burnout threshold is and arrange work to suit. Mine is about six to eight weeks of working solid, so 27 years after school I still need half term! I aim to take at least a couple of days off at around that time, otherwise it will take longer to bounce back."

Craig Wright, StrayGoat Writing Services

"If your brain says no and deadlines allow, listen to your brain. Take a break (or the rest of the day off), do something fun or playful, and let your brain recharge. You'll get the work done quicker and better if you don't force it, and your brain will thank you for it."

@MegRFreelance

"Take a lunch break and have a cut-off time when you'll stop work. It's easy to keep going and going on work stuff, which wouldn't happen in an office. Give yourself a 'home time' and then do non-work-related stuff once you're done for the day."

Rose Crompton, content marketer and copywriter

"Tips that work for me:
- Get showered and dressed.
- No work in bed or on the sofa.
- Take a lunch break (ideally going outside).
- Set a time to stop working and stick to it when possible.
- Socialise with colleagues: celebrate wins and commiserate lows."

@edcallowwrites

"The best thing I ever did for myself is to maintain office hours. They're on my email signature and in every client contract I give out. I make clients aware that I won't respond to messages outside of these hours, so I get proper rest time away from work."

@DragonAyres

"Be firm and clear with clients about when **you** can get something done rather than letting them set the deadlines. This helps keep a sense of control over your work. Things are rarely as urgent as clients say they are."

@flickwild

- "Schedule in burnout-busting activities – such as a walk or gym session – and make them appointments with yourself in your calendar so you stick to them.
- Under-promise, over-deliver. Don't say you can do something by tomorrow, say it'll take two to three days then deliver early if you can.
- Raise your prices."

@annabeljfay

"As well as learning to say no, I would also add to take email off your phone so that you are able to fully switch off when you are not working. If you have time to plan ahead monthly, this also helps reduce overwhelm for me."

Ruth Buckingham, marketing consultant

"Follow these simple steps, and you and your business will be happier and more successful:

- Roll your shoulders down at least twice a day. They're up to your ears.
- Take a full lunch break.
- Take time away from the screen.
- Don't feel guilty about taking time for things you love.
- Do some regular yoga or Pilates."

Mark Grainger, copywriter

"I experienced burnout in 2004 and made some big life changes as a result. I was teaching full time and struggled with never having time to be quiet and alone. I gave up my job and worked in a bookshop, where we were allowed to choose a book and keep it in the staff room to read in our breaks. The silence was wonderful as everyone was reading!

"My tip is to stop working and take a minimum 30 minutes to one-hour lunch break every working day. I worked too many jobs where the lunch break disappeared, and food was eaten on the move."

@SunAtelier

"I take my mind off work or meeting deadlines. I take a shower or maybe take a walk. Music helps, too. Or sometimes I just go out to a bar or an eatery and watch people around."

@meetoluwafemi

"Once a week, make time to enjoy being freelance. Take a lunchtime yoga class, run errands, or finish early to meet a friend."

@sallymfoxwrites

"I don't feel pressured to start my working day at 9am. I'll start closer to 11am and work later when everyone else has logged off! It gives me the morning to focus on 'me things' and chores, so that I can relax into work later in the day."

Annie Thorpe, Thorpe Writing Services

"Learn to turn your wifi off. Don't answer emails out of hours and don't feel you have to answer everyone immediately."

@charli_says

MYTH EIGHT

"Once I have enough experience,
failure won't bother me."

The reality

Imposter syndrome can get in your way if you let it

You can't read an article about being freelance without coming across the term 'imposter syndrome'.

If you're not familiar with the concept, it's that nagging feeling that you're inadequate, incompetent, and generally undeserving of success. It can occur whether you're employed or self-employed, but according to my own experience and the conversations I had with other freelancers while writing this book, it certainly runs deep in the world of self-employment.

Sometimes imposter syndrome shows up as a mean voice in your head: "You think you can succeed as a freelancer? Who are you kidding?" or "You can't charge that! Who do you think you are?!".

Sometimes it's the crippling anxiety that accompanies the start of a project for a new client. The fear of failure, of disappointing people, and of not being good enough.

Sometimes it's a feeling that you've been faking it and you'll be exposed as a fraud at any moment. That you don't deserve success, and you've only got where you are today by sheer guts and chance.

Imposter syndrome has a lot in common with self-doubt. It stems from a fear of being found out or not measuring up – despite evidence to the contrary. You know very well what you're doing. On a good day, you might even admit that you're pretty good at it. Yet still imposter syndrome lurks around the corner, waiting to stop you in your tracks when you least expect it.

The term imposter syndrome was coined in the 1970s by Suzanne Imes and Pauline Rose Clance. Rather than being a personality trait, it's a reaction to circumstances, and is described as "the inability to believe that one's success is deserved or has been legitimately achieved as a result of one's efforts or skills".

While early research into imposter syndrome focused on high-achieving women, it's now understood to impact both men and women – something author and strategist, Megan Dalla-Camina, confirms: "We all suffer from imposter syndrome. I've known senior men in business who struggle with it day in, day out, including general managers running billion-dollar companies and speakers who command audiences in the thousands. It really can affect anyone."

According to research[1], 76% of freelancers don't feel talented enough – and the conversations I had in the process of writing this book appeared to back that up. The more freelancers I spoke to, the more I became convinced that, deep down, we **all** feel like we're winging it from time to time.

There's a great scene in the popular TV show, *Parks and Recreation*, in which two characters talk about imposter syndrome. Andy confesses to his partner, April, that he's feeling totally in over his head with his new job. April responds, "I'm going to tell you a secret about everyone else's job: no one knows what they're doing... deep down, everyone is just faking it until they figure it out."

Even the late poet Maya Angelou was once quoted as saying, "I have written 11 books, but each time I think, 'uh oh, they're going to find out now. I've run a game on everybody and they're going to find me out.'"

Becoming unstuck

The problem with imposter syndrome is that it can hold you back if you don't get it in check. Self-doubt keeps you firmly in your comfort zone, stops you taking risks, and prevents you from doing things that are good for your business.

For me, it was launching my own newsletter.

I'd been writing newsletters for my clients for over 20 years, yet somehow writing my own was too big, too scary a prospect, too much of a commitment...

If I didn't do it, I couldn't fail – right?

I came up with the idea of my *Clever Copy Club* newsletter[2] at the start of 2016. I knew I wanted to share helpful tips that anyone could use to improve their writing, rather than hammering home the benefits of working with a copywriter.

Yet it was never the right moment. "I don't have the time to write a newsletter!" I told myself. "I'm already too busy. I can't handle all the work it'll bring in."

Why was I stuck? Simple. It was nothing more than paralysing fear. Being a copywriter with perfectionist tendencies may be great from my clients' point of view; from my perspective, not so much.

Taking the leap

Mailchimp training completed and an unfeasible amount of procrastination later, I finally hit the send button on the first ever issue of my newsletter. Off it went, winging its electronic way to over 600 people... and I can't even begin to describe the terror.

What if everyone hates it? What if I become known as the copywriter with the rubbish newsletter? What if everyone unsubscribes?! How will I live with the shame?!

But you know what? I survived. I'd even go as far as to say I felt good. I wasn't expecting miracles – the miracle was just getting it done – but the risk paid off. Two days later, I had:

- a 48.6% open rate

- an 8.2% click rate

- six meetings booked

- two confirmed pieces of work

- no less than 24 "well done – I love it!" emails and tweets

Okay, so they weren't mind-blowing results, it wasn't perfect, but **it was good enough**.

For you, self-doubt may show up as a mean, nagging voice that holds you back from pitching for big-budget projects. Maybe it prevents you from putting up your prices ("No one's going to pay that to work with you!"). Or perhaps it stops you stepping up to talk about your business at a conference or event.

Whatever is getting in your way or keeping you stuck, remember – it doesn't have to be life-changing or world-class or revolutionary. There will never be a perfect time, and you will never be truly ready.

So just do it.

The perfection connection

Imposter syndrome's big sister is perfectionism – and it's easy to see why.

Perfectionists are known for setting unrealistic goals that anyone would struggle to achieve. We then wallow in worry, self-doubt, and self-loathing (just me?) when we believe we're not working hard enough – or that we aren't good enough – to succeed.

Here's a thing: you **are** worthy, you **do** deserve this, and you **are** good enough.

Most of the time – at least on the good days – you know you've got this. Yet still the doubt creeps in. It's all part of being human. And you know what? It's not all bad. After all, a little self-doubt prevents us from becoming arrogant, self-important, and egotistical (no one wants that, right?).

What's more, it's entirely normal.

You know what else is normal? The fear of success.

Yes, you read that right.

Often what we think is a fear of failure is actually a fear of success. To quote American author, Marianne Williamson: "Our deepest fear is not that we are inadequate. Our deepest fear is that we are powerful beyond measure".

We fear the unknown and shy away from change as a result. We're so comfortable in our own familiar, well-defined bubble that the thought of changing our lives – even for the better – is scary.

What does success look like? How does it feel? What if we don't like it when we get there?

Whether you're scared of success or afraid of failure, there are steps you can take to tackle these feelings. Let's look at some of the ways in which you can kick self-doubt and imposter syndrome to the kerb.

The advice

Don't let the fear of failure hold you back

Imagine you've been invited to deliver a talk at a networking event. When the day comes, the adrenaline starts to flow and the old 'fight or flight' response kicks in. The flurry of butterflies that descends when we step outside our comfort zone reminds us we're alive.

Any time my children have had to do something brave and uncomfortable – like performing in a school play or interviewing for a job – I've given them the same advice:

"Remember that being nervous and being excited feel just the same. Tell your brain you're excited to be doing something new – something brave and bold – and you're more likely to enjoy it, and to do well."

The more TED Talks and podcasts I listen to, the more I become convinced that everyone gets an attack of the nerves before speaking in public – even the most seasoned presenters.

HOW IS IT FOR YOU?

A case in point is Dr Andy Cope. Andy studied happiness for 12 years and now delivers keynote speeches on the subject to audiences around the world. "I deliver and teach wellbeing, yet before I go on stage I'm racked with nerves and panic and wonder why the hell I'm doing this, every single time. 'Ooh, doctor of happiness, people won't take you seriously. Who are you to stand on stage and tell people about wellbeing?'

"Everyone thinks they're the only one that's terrified of stepping outside their comfort zone, but everyone has the same insecurities as you do. The realisation that we **all** feel uncomfortable, and that we're all waiting to be found out is, in itself, quite comforting. It's perfectly okay not to be okay – it's part of the human condition.

"Ultimately, no one really cares how you feel; they're all worried about you judging them. So be the one with confidence – and if you're not feeling confident, pretend. Stand taller and put a smile on your face. It changes your body language, which massively affects how you feel."

So, don't let doubt and negative feelings prevent you from achieving the things you're capable of. You're in charge. Show them who's boss.

Dealing with self-doubt

Being aware of the situations and circumstances that trigger self-doubt can help you feel more equipped to deal with them.

A few simple strategies can help you keep self-doubt and imposter syndrome in check:

1. *Accept mistakes*

2. *Stop comparing yourself*

3. *Keep talking*

4. *Reward yourself for taking risks*

5. *Celebrate your successes*

6. *List the things you're good at*

Let's look at each of these strategies in more depth.

1. Accept mistakes

Everyone makes mistakes: it's a fact of life. Without trying new things – and without failure – we can't grow.

We try, we fail, we learn, we grow.

When I searched for quotes about learning from mistakes, I found words of wisdom from everyone from Bill Gates and Dale Carnegie to Eleanor Roosevelt and Naomi Campbell. This quote from the writer, Neil Gaiman, is my favourite:

> "I hope that in this year to come, you make mistakes. Because if you are making mistakes, then you are making new things, trying new things, learning, living, pushing yourself, changing the world. You're doing things you've never done before, and more importantly, you're doing something.

"So that's my wish for you, and all of us, and my wish for myself. Make new mistakes. Make glorious, amazing mistakes. Make mistakes nobody's ever made before. Don't freeze, don't stop, don't worry that it isn't good enough, or it isn't perfect. Whatever it is: art, or love, or work, or family, or life."

Mistakes are a vital part of the learning process, so embrace them.

2. Stop comparing yourself

"Comparison is the thief of joy," as Teddy Roosevelt once said. Sure enough, if you look hard enough, there will always be someone who appears to be doing more and doing it better. Comparison can lead to disappointment, dissatisfaction, and doubt – so stop doing it! As long as you're happy with how far you've come and what you've achieved, it doesn't matter what anyone else is up to.

3. Keep talking

Fears and doubts have a way of intensifying when you keep them to yourself. You're not the only person who suffers from self-doubt, and you're not alone – but it sure as hell can feel that way! Try opening up to a trusted friend or colleague. You may be surprised to find they feel the same. Talking about your feelings can help to normalise them.

4. Reward yourself for taking risks

Challenging projects bring opportunities to develop your skills and grow as a person. Sometimes the self-esteem boost and mindset shift that comes from just damn well doing it are all the reward you need.

I'm not suggesting you celebrate with a slap-up meal after bungee-jumping off the Empire State Building. (Is that even a thing? I doubt it.) Instead, recognise and reward yourself for the actions that take you outside your comfort zone. Ultimately, even the smallest steps can make a big difference to your success as a freelancer.

5. Celebrate your successes

Stop chalking your wins up to chance and coincidence. Instead, recognise every little success for the achievement it is. A client wrote you a review on LinkedIn – brilliant! You talked to someone you didn't know at a networking event – yay! You won a new client – go you!

Reflecting on your achievements is an important part of the learning process. Identify the things that went well **and** the things that could have gone better. Apply this learning to other projects so you can do more of the former and less of the latter.

Reaching the end of a large or challenging project can be a good time to do this, but any time is a good time for reflection.

6. List the things you're good at

Pin it to your wall if you need to and read it often, together with your favourite customer reviews and testimonials. Give yourself credit for how much you've accomplished, how far you've come, and how much you've learned along the way – especially the lessons you learned the hard way. Things may not have gone the way you expected, but you took a risk and grew as a result. That's worth celebrating.

The importance of learning

By adopting some or all of these strategies you'll be better equipped to handle the wobbles and insecurity that can get in your way as a freelancer.

But those nagging feelings of self-doubt aren't always a bad thing. They have another vital function: they alert us to gaps in our knowledge, so we can do something about them.

We freelancers are solely responsible for our own professional and personal development. According to Leapers' research, 45% of solo workers find it stressful finding both the time and the money for training and development – yet it's vital to stay up-to-date and informed if you want to succeed.

Things change daily in this digital age, and it's important to keep up with industry news, developments in social media, and the latest tools and technology.

Not sure how something works? Buy a book on the subject, take a workshop, or watch YouTube tutorials until you're familiar with the process. Learn new skills by enrolling in local or online courses.

Stay on top of current trends in your field by reading relevant articles and following influential leaders on platforms such as

LinkedIn and Twitter. Ask colleagues, peers, and your online community for recommended reads or podcasts, or for inspiring people to follow.

Consider joining the professional body that represents your industry. As well as sharing thought-provoking content to keep you abreast of the latest trends, many professional associations offer formal learning and development, such as conferences, training sessions, and webinars.

Struggling to know how to take your business to the next level, or failing to stick to your goals? Join a mastermind group or training programme or find a mentor or coach to provide ongoing support and accountability.

Events such as conferences and training days are a great way to ramp up your learning. What's more, they have the added benefit of keeping you in touch with likeminded people and helping you to feel less isolated and more connected. Take notes, type them up so they sink in, read and reread them.

Speaking of reading... read voraciously. Read about your trade, about business, about psychology. Anything that feeds your imagination, inspires you, and helps you to be a better freelancer – and a better person.

Don't enjoy reading, or can't find the time? There's still plenty you can do. Subscribe to podcasts or watch TED Talks or industry experts share their wisdom online, or consider joining a service such as Audible or Blinkist so you can listen to business or personal development books when you're in the car, or cooking dinner.

While the fear of failure never really goes away, it's only by going outside of our comfort zone and risking disappointment that we grow as individuals. The only true failure is becoming complacent.

So, keep learning, stay curious, and remember – sometimes good enough really **is** good enough.

---

1   How are we doing? Leapers research into freelancing and mental health: leapers.co/huru/report/

2   You can subscribe to my Clever Copy Club newsletter at https://mailchi.mp/ ff28d142d926/gmbsignup

Time out...

Revisit the list of ways to tackle self-doubt in this chapter and spend some time on the following:

- **Reflect on what you've achieved.**
  I like to end every day by reflecting on three things I've achieved. Sometimes those successes are significant: perhaps I won a new client or met a challenging deadline. Other times they're small wins: I made a new connection, paid my invoices, or had a good chat with a client.

  You might prefer to do this in more detail at the end of each week or month, or perhaps when you finish a piece of work or project. Consider keeping a positivity journal, so you can revisit and reflect on your achievements any time self-doubt creeps in and you need a confidence boost.

- **Make a list of the things you're good at.**
  Use coloured pens and fancy lettering if you feel like getting creative. Pin your list somewhere you'll see it every day. Read it often and add to it regularly.

FREELANCER FEEDBACK...

"I envy anyone who doesn't have the fear gene when it comes to self-employment. Imposter syndrome held me back for so long. Who am I to be doing this? What if I get found out? Making friends with the little voice in my head was the best thing I did. That little voice is just doing its job and keeping you safe. Once you reassure it that all will be well you can take it along for the ride. Sure, it shouts up every now and then but the more you step out of your comfort zone, the quieter that chatterbox becomes."

Tracey Tait, marketing coach and trainer

"I'm not naturally someone who suffers from imposter syndrome – I prefer to call it 'winging it'. There have been times in my business when I've felt out of my depth, but we will forever restrict our potential if we only do things we're completely comfortable with.

"There's a lot of talk about imposter syndrome these days, and I think if we're not careful we can talk ourselves into it. I've found that if you just go for it then amazing, unexpected things can happen. You just have to have a bit of nerve in the first place."

Sophie Bradshaw, writing coach and
editor of GoWrite Magazine

"Imposter syndrome is a big problem for me. It makes me feel inadequate and anxious, causes me to question my success and – what's worse – it stops me from doing things I want to do. Sometimes it comes from nowhere and completely overwhelms me; other times it can be a result of something that's happened during the day, like losing a client, or failing to win a job. Negative thoughts build up, and I find myself in a spiral of self-doubt.

"It's much more of a problem when you're self-employed. When you work in an office you chat about your fears and doubts with your colleagues, they reassure you and the doubt goes away. I partnered with a friend to set up a Facebook group and networking event to provide support for other women in my position, for this reason. Having other people you can talk to makes you feel a lot less alone."

Sam Johnstone, virtual assistant and co-founder of
Women's Informative Networking

"With eight failed businesses came a natural fear of failure. It didn't help that, seven years ago, I was laid off for the second time in three years. I knew something had to change, and I was determined not to let fear hold me back. After I signed on a significant client, I knew that if I could find a few more, I could make self-employment work, but it'd be tough – especially since I don't have a degree in my industry (I'm completely self-taught). But I worked hard for months, and after a couple of years, my current business ended up being my most successful."

Kim Siever, writer and editor

"It doesn't stop being scary. Learn, network, expand your contacts, be business minded for the practical bits, be flexible, be creative, be nice and work with nice people, be confident, get paid, have a work–life balance!"

Verity S R Smith, museum curator and writer

"Imposter syndrome results in the feeling that we aren't good enough. If you're not careful, it has a tendency to travel with you on your journey. How do you prevent it from stopping you in your tracks? Have the mindset that you're good enough to do the required work. Ultimately, doing the work is all that matters when it comes to achieving results."

Paul Healey, author and business coach

"I've learned that if you don't keep current on the latest trends, you will soon become irrelevant. Things are changing daily, and I've found that investing in my personal and professional development always pays dividends. That's why I continually scour the web for ways to improve my writing and marketing skills. I learn from other freelancers, as well as from businesses and professionals from a variety of industries. I read books, blogs, articles, and complete training courses to hone my skills regularly. I probably learn at least one new thing every day."

Kaylene Mathews, writer and blogger

"Imposter syndrome can limit our courage to go after new opportunities, explore potential areas of interest, and put ourselves out there in a meaningful way. Voicing your fears in coaching, with a mentor, or in a safe peer group helps to normalize the feelings and to remind you you're not alone. Listing your achievements, skills, and successes reminds you of your value and helps to improve confidence levels."

Megan Dalla-Camina, author and strategist

"Self-employment has shifted my relationship to work. I now find joy in my work in a way I didn't before. I've rediscovered my love of writing, tried new skills I never thought I'd be any good at and learned that fulfilment comes from listening to your intrinsic motivators rather than chasing superficial goals.

"I've finally understood that you can be good at your job and not have to keep trying to prove that fact by working yourself into the ground. For example, you can take the day off for your birthday – something I never did when I worked in-house – and not feel guilty about it."

Anna Codrea-Rado, journalist and
co-host of Is This Working? podcast

Conclusion

Thomas Jefferson once said, "It seems the harder I work, the more luck I have."

But when it comes to building a successful freelance career, it's not just about how **hard** you work – it's also about how **smart** you work.

Can you be smart enough to ask for help with the things you don't enjoy, and to tackle the isolation that comes with the territory?

Can you be smart enough to treat your freelance career as a business, and to invest in your brand and your own personal development?

Can you be smart enough to know your own value, to set boundaries, and to say no to the work that just doesn't feel right?

And can you be smart enough to be money savvy – to prioritise your pension and protection, and put money aside for the inevitable tax bills?

If the posts on platforms such as LinkedIn are anything to go by, we live in a bravado culture where busyness is regarded as a measure of our success, and the number of hours we feel compelled to work during evenings and weekends are worn as a badge of honour.

But that shouldn't be the case.

Success isn't about how much you earn, the car you drive, or the number of exotic holidays you take.

True success is about balance.

It's about feeling fulfilled and inspired by a job you love, and working with people who encourage and support you. It includes allocating time to reflect, restore and relax.

Most of all, success prioritises your wellbeing and mental health. Because only by setting boundaries and taking care of your emotional resilience will you be the best freelancer – and the best **you** – you can be.

My wish is that by talking honestly and openly about the risk of overwhelm and burnout, I'll have helped you to avoid it in some small way.

In summary...

By getting an insight into the joy and pain that pave the way to freelance success, you've learned:

- Being a solo worker doesn't mean going it alone. We **all** need to feel connected.

- Trying to do everything yourself is the fast train to burnout. Don't be afraid to ask for help.

- You won't succeed until you take your business seriously. Adopt the right mindset, and invest for success.

- Know (and charge) your worth. If you don't value yourself, your clients won't, either.

- If something feels wrong, it probably is. Tune in to your instinct, and learn to say no.

- Be prepared for some hard graft. Value your time off, and pay yourself first!

- Yes, freelance life can be tough, but it's okay not to be okay.

- Don't let the fear of failure hold you back. Only by going outside your comfort zone do you learn and grow.

I hope that adopting my tried and tested strategies enables you to supercharge your progress on the quest for freelance success.

Good luck!

Sarah x

Next steps

If you've enjoyed this book, I have one small favour to ask: **please** pop online and **leave a review** on Amazon.

Each positive review helps to make the time, love and effort that went into this book worthwhile, and I'd be so grateful to know how you've benefited from the advice it contains.

Once you've left an online review...

- Help me reach as many freelancers as possible by spreading the word and telling your self-employed friends and colleagues about this book.

- Use the hashtag **#survivalskillsforfreelancers** to share a photo of the book with your favourite quote for the chance to be retweeted or featured! You'll find me as **@STEcopywriting** on Twitter and Instagram.

- If you'd like to stay in touch, **sign up** to my Clever Copy Club newsletter. You'll find a sign-up box on my website for monthly email updates.

- To find out more about what I do day-to-day as a copywriter, head over to my **website** – sarahtownsendeditorial.co.uk – or **email me** at hello@sarahtownsend editorial.co.uk

- You're welcome to connect with me on **LinkedIn** (linkedin.com/in/sarahtownsendeditorial). I'd love to know which part of *Survival Skills for Freelancers* you enjoyed most, so pop that in your message.

Above all, start putting my tips into action, and let me know how you get on!

References

Recommended books

If you want to learn to improve your mindset, become more successful, sell more stuff or market your business better, here are some recommendations to get you started:

Mindset and success

Influence: The Psychology of Persuasion: Robert B Cialdini

The Seven Habits of Highly Effective People: Stephen R Covey

Start With Why and *Find Your Why:* Simon Sinek

Grit: Angela Duckworth

Mindset: Dr Carol S Dweck

The Slight Edge: Jeff Olson

Company Of One: Paul Jarvis

Sales and marketing

Copywriting Made Simple: Tom Albrighton

Anti-Sell: Steve Morgan

They Ask, You Answer: Marcus Sheridan

How to Write Better Copy: Steve Harrison

Everybody Writes: Your Go-To Guide to Creating Ridiculously Good Content: Ann Handley

Persuasive Copywriting: Andy Maslen

Read Me: 10 Lessons for Writing Great Copy: Roger Horberry and Gyles Lingwood

Resources

Online communities

Freelance Heroes
facebook.com/groups/freelanceheroes/
freelance-heroes.com/

Freelancing Females
facebook.com/groups/freelancingfems/
freelancingfemales.com

Being Freelance
facebook.com/groups/beingfreelance
beingfreelance.com

Doing It For The Kids
facebook.com/groups/DIFTK/
doingitforthekids.net

Leapers
leapers.co

Mental health and wellbeing

Mind: mind.org.uk

Mental Health First Aid (MHFA): there are MHFA programmes in many countries around the world. Details at: mhfainternational.org

Mental Health Foundation: mentalhealth.org.uk

Minds@Work: mindsatworkmovement.com

NHS 5 steps to mental wellbeing: nhs.uk/conditions/stress-anxiety-depression/improve-mental-wellbeing/

Contracts and legal

The Association of Independent Professionals and the Self-Employed (IPSE): ipse.co.uk

The following websites are a good starting point for information on contracts:

Simply docs: simply-docs.co.uk/home

Three Wise Monkeys: stuffandnonsense.co.uk/projects/contract-killer/

Legalo: legalo.co.uk/

Podcasts and publications

Being Freelance: podcast

Freelance Feels: podcast

Doing It For The Kids: podcast

Is This Working?: podcast

Freelance Pod: podcast

The Homeworker: magazine: thehomeworker.com

Money, tax and what to charge

Find an independent financial adviser (IFA): unbiased.co.uk

Freelancing Females rate sheet: freelancingfemales.com/rates

Payment on account: gov.uk/understand-self-assessment-bill/payments-on-account

Pensions for freelancers: moneyadviceservice.org.uk/en/articles/pensions-for-the-self-employed

Free, impartial money advice: moneyadviceservice.org.uk/en

Personality profiling

Myers-Briggs Type Indicator® (MBTI): myersbriggs.org

DiSC® personality profiling: discprofile.com

The Four Tendencies quiz: quiz.gretchenrubin.com

Acknowledgements

I spoke to many colleagues and work friends in the process of writing *Survival Skills for Freelancers*. I couldn't have done this without their encouragement, support and advice.

Huge thanks to the following:

- Those whose brains I picked about the process of self-publishing: Tom Albrighton, Simon Clayton, John Espirian, Claire Jennison, Steve Morgan, Jonathan Pollinger, Robin Waite and Gill Wyatt.

- Simon Blake for my fabulous foreword and support.

- Richard Bell and Karen Mitchell from Maple Rock Design for my cover design and landing page.

- Catherine Williams for page layout.

- Rebecca Lowe for proofreading and copy editing.

- Everyone from within my freelance network – both on and offline – who allowed me to include their quotes, advice and wisdom.

- Special thanks to Dr Andy Cope, April Doty, Steve Folland, Louise Goss, Anna Gunning, Matthew Knight, Nick Parker, Graeme Piper, Jenny Stallard, George and Amy Townsend, and Jez Wallace.